FLAVOR TRAIN

CHUCK'S FLAVOR TRAIN

CHUCK'S FLAVOR TRAIN

YOUR TICKET TO SMOKIN' HOT BARBECUE

CHUCK MATTO

weldonowen

Dedication

Food isn't just something we eat. It's a physical expression of life and all that comes with it . . . love, care, joy, and togetherness. The good, the bad . . . the beautiful, and the ugly, along with everything in between. That idea might sound poetic or even a little over the top to some. But if you were ever lucky enough to have shared a meal with my mom, Regina Matto, you'd know exactly what I mean. You see, my mom didn't just feed people. She healed, celebrated, supported, and connected with them through every dish. It's in her honor that I dedicate this book to her and her memory. My mom, the woman who taught me that food has the power to change lives.

My mom gave me the greatest gift of all: life. At eight months old, I was adopted. *I* was the kid she chose. Later, she chose again: my younger sister, Zee. But she didn't just adopt us, she dedicated her entire life to us. To me, to Zee, to my older siblings, Lisa, Jenny, and Joe, and to more than fifty foster children who found comfort, stability, and love under her roof. My mom is living proof that angels walk among us, and that the world can be changed through nothing more than consistent, selfless love. Even if she had done nothing else in her life, I would be proof that food, and the love that comes with it, can change a life. A simple conversation over a meal with my dad led to their decision to adopt me. That meal gave me a future. She gave me a chance and then filled my life with more love than I could've ever hoped for.

Growing up, family dinner was the highlight of my day. No matter how rough things got. Bad days at school, scrapes from street football, drama with friends, I knew I could count on the smell of Mom's pot roast or spaghetti and meatballs to instantly lift my spirits. I'd be sprinting home by six p.m. sharp, leaving my buddies confused. "But, Chuck, don't you want to keep playing?" they'd shout. "Uhhhhh, no . . . it's dinnertime," I'd reply, as if the question itself were absurd. More often than not, those same friends ended up joining us around the table. Because my mom wasn't just *my* mom, she was everyone's. She welcomed teammates, classmates, neighbors, and foster kids with the same love she gave her own children. If someone was going through a tough time, they had a seat at our table.

If we were wiped out from a summer day shooting hoops, she had sandwiches and Capri-Suns ready. When my brother Joe came home from college to visit (well, mostly to do laundry, if I'm being real), she made sure the whole family knew we were having a feast! And the *holidays*?!?! That was a sensation of sensory overload: the smells, the laughter, the love. Those meals were the stage and backdrop for some of the best memories of my life.

So many of those meals are remembered, not just for how delicious and comforting they were, but for what they meant. Around that table, I watched my mom comfort and guide foster kids through difficult transitions, help friends through heartbreak, and quietly support my sister and then my dad through cancer. I saw her instill confidence in people who had lost it. I witnessed meals become the catalyst for healing, forgiveness, even transformation. I saw how food led to sobriety, second chances, and new beginnings. A dinner conversation sparked the adoption of a child, giving them a life they never imagined. My mom's meals weren't just food, they were love, hope, and connection served on a plate.

And through all of it, she cooked with such ease. She never followed strict recipes or measured obsessively. She just *knew*. She trusted her instincts, cooked with love, and paid attention to the people she was feeding. That's something I've carried into my own cooking style. I go with my gut. I taste and adjust. I cook for who's in front of me. If a dish needs more salt, I add it. If my daughter's eating and the heat's too high, I scale it back. Because every dish is a reflection of you, and if you put care and love into it, people can feel it. And if you don't? Trust me, they'll feel that too.

More than anything, my mom taught me that a good meal can make people feel like family. Around her table, you talked, laughed, spilled drinks, and made memories. That's the kind of cooking I want to honor in this book. The kind that turns meals into moments, and strangers into family. I used to say, "Food is love." But I've come to realize *love* is love. Food was just one of the many ways my mom chose to share hers.

I love you, Momma . . . thank you for everything.

Spread Love
Do Dope

Contents

CHAPTER 4

SEAFOOD

The Wharf Wagon

CHAPTER 5

RIBS

Trackside Racks

CHAPTER 6

LAMB, GAME, AND MORE

Exotic Riders

CHAPTER 7

COCKTAILS

The Lounge Car

Welcome Aboard

ABOUT ME

I'm a lot of things. A husband, a father, a son. A fat guy who loves food, a 49ers Faithful, a proud San Francisco Giants fan, and an unapologetic hater of the Dodgers. I'm a proud Californian with Bay Area roots and a kid at heart still chasing his dreams. But above all else, before the BBQ, the cooking videos, the social media, or the TV shows, I'm a husband and a father. That's the most important part of who I am.

My wife is my rock. My partner, my best friend, my manager, my therapist, and sometimes my designated adult when I drink too much or double-book myself. She's been there through every up and down, every detour, every crazy idea. She sees things in me I don't always see in myself, and I truly don't know where I'd be without her . . . but I know it wouldn't be anywhere good. She's the glue that holds it all together when I feel like I'm coming undone. And then there's my daughter, my princess: Amaya Marie. You've shown me what love really means and reminded me, every single day, what this life is about. The day you were born is burned into my soul forever. I can't imagine a life without you, because that wouldn't be a life. Your personality, your fire, your laughter, your wild and beautiful soul . . . there aren't words big enough to describe what you mean to me. You light up every room you walk into. Like I always tell you: never change. Keep being you. Share that heart of yours with the world and keep smiling. Being your dad is the best thing I've ever done and I'm so proud of you.

The journeys and adventures I've had with the two of them, my girls, are the kind of things I used to dream about as a kid. We've laughed, we've cried, we've danced around the kitchen, and we've eaten like royalty on a peasant's budget. We've made memories that I'll carry with me forever. I'm not perfect, not even close. I've made my share of mistakes. But I try every day to be a better man, for them. To give them the world, or at least the tastiest parts of it. They are my "why." They are the reason I grind, the reason I create, the reason I keep showing up. I know how lucky I am to do what I do. But more than that, I know how lucky I am to have them.

As long as I can remember, I've loved food. And let's be honest, you don't build a body like mine overnight. It takes years of dedication to steak, pasta, and cheap liquor. A slow simmer, not a flash-fry. But beyond the jokes and jiggly bits, food has always been more than a meal. It's been my compass. My comfort. My connection to the world. Growing up, food was a big deal in my family. My mom's dinners were the heartbeat of our house. And my dad's "BBQ" (char-grilled ribs cooked on a gas grill) might've been sacrilege to purists, but to me, they were magic. Meals weren't just meals. They were events. They were the thing I looked forward to most.

My dad still tells the story of me, four years old in Lake Tahoe, sitting in a restaurant and confidently ordering baby octopus. He asked, "Are you sure that's what you want?" and I just nodded. The plate arrived: tentacles, suckers, all of it! And I dove in like I'd been waiting my whole life. I ate every last bite like it was my job. I wasn't just eating, I was performing. That was my moment. At four years old, I wasn't scared of food. I respected it. I was curious about it. I wanted to understand it. And that curiosity never left me. If it looked good, I ate it. If it smelled funky, I sniffed deeper. If someone told me, "You probably won't like that," I took it as a challenge. That Lake Tahoe trip wasn't just a family vacation: It was my origin story. The moment I realized food wasn't something to be picky about. It was an adventure. And I wanted in.

One of my earliest food obsessions came from a daytime infomercial for something called the Turbo Cooker. The type of fever-dream commercial you could only catch before *Jenny Jones*. It was this wild contraption: part wok, part pressure cooker. It was like a glorified spaceship that could cook an entire meal in a pan. I had to have it. I laid down the psychological groundwork like a baby David Blaine until my mom finally caved and got it for me. She had one rule: "Don't tell your dad." Say less! Deal. A few days later it arrived. My mom took me to Browns Valley Market and helped me grab everything I needed. New York strip steak, broccoli, onions, soy sauce, and the fancy part: red wine. I cooked it all up using the Turbo Cooker, following the instructions like scripture. Twenty minutes later, I was serving steak and broccoli in red wine sauce to a crew of seven- and eight-year-old neighborhood kids like I was running a fine-dining pop-up. I was ten. It was absurd. It was over the top. And I loved it.

Food wasn't just about cooking . . . it was everything around it. The personalities, the energy, the vibe. And no one embodied that more than Emeril Lagasse. I was mesmerized. The way he moved, talked, and cooked. He didn't just cook, he *performed*. One hand tossing garlic, the other stirring sauce, all while shouting *"BAM!"* and hyping up the crowd like a damn rock star. I'd sit there glued to the screen, hopped up on Rice Krispies Treats and Hawaiian Punch, completely entranced. He made food *fun*. He didn't look like a Hollywood chef . . . he looked like someone's cool uncle who could throw down and crack jokes at the same time. For a big kid like me, who loved to eat and make people laugh, that meant everything. He made cooking approachable and exciting. He taught me that flavor comes from energy, from *being yourself*, from putting love and a little chaos into every dish. Emeril wasn't just a TV chef. He was the first person who made me believe there might be a place for someone like me in the food world.

In college, while most people were learning about economics or existentialism, I was learning about tri-tip and teriyaki. Some students pulled all-nighters studying for exams. I pulled all-nighters at the frat house with boys getting blackout. I found a crew that liked to live like I did eating big, steady smoking, drinking heavy, and enjoying every second of it. Friends like Ross and Bryce were right there with me. We threw backyard dinners like they were Food Network productions, except instead of truffles and foie gras, it was Bud's Custom Meats and a couple 30-racks. We'd fire up the Weber Kettle, throw on whatever protein we could afford, and let the smoke do its thing while Bay Area rap rattled the windows. Lagunitas in hand, smoke in the air, laughter everywhere . . . it didn't get better than that. We weren't trained chefs. We were broke and hungry, with questionable cookware and zero formal technique. But we cooked with love. With energy. With passion. We learned how to build flavor, how to feed people, how to create moments around food. Looking back, those backyard meals were my first taste of what this life could really be.

After college, I took a job at Hanna Boys Center, a group home for at-risk youth. I lived on-site for three-and-a-half-day shifts and was responsible for everything from meds to mentorship. But the part I loved most was cooking. We'd plan meals, take the boys shopping, and cook breakfast and dinner every day. It was chaotic, loud, and messy, but it was also perfect.

Dinnertime was sacred. It was where the tension from the day melted away. Where jokes flew, stories were told, and sometimes, yeah, farts cleared the room. One night we had a rib-eating contest. I housed twenty-seven ribs and sat at the table, victorious, sweating like Shaq in game seven. I was delirious from sodium, meat-drunk, and crying laughing with a group of kids who just needed someone to show up for them. Food was the bridge.

In 2012, I met the woman who would eventually become my wife, and like any self-respecting man with a passion for food and zero game, I tried to impress her the only way I knew how: by cooking. I rolled up to her condo armed with a cheap cut of steak, a box of pasta, and a bottle of wine I *thought* was fancy (it was probably Carlo Rossi, if I'm being real). I was nervous as hell. Her kitchen was . . . humble, to say the least. One dull knife, a warped frying pan, and a stovetop that ran hotter than the surface of the sun. But I made it work. I cooked that steak like it was filet mignon, tossed the pasta in whatever sauce I could whip up, and poured the wine like I was sommelier of the year. It wasn't a perfect meal by any means, but it was ours. We sat on the couch, laughed, ate, and talked like we had known each other for years. That dinner wasn't just the beginning of our relationship; it was the start of something real. A little reminder that the most meaningful meals in life aren't always about the ingredients, but who you share them with and the memories you make.

Later, when we moved into our tiny apartment in Santa Rosa, the Grocery Outlet downtown on Fourth Street became our go-to. And I don't just mean we shopped there. I mean that place *kept us alive*. We were two broke young adults trying to figure out life, rent, and what the hell we could cook up for twenty dollars. Grocery Outlet was like a hidden treasure chest for hungry folks with imagination. I remember walking through the meat section like it was a Vegas buffet and finding cuts of meat I didn't think we could ever afford. Lamb shanks, pork shoulder, whole chickens, sometimes even tri-tip, all for prices that made me do a double take. There were days I'd walk in and find a two-pack of lamb shanks for eight dollars. *Eight. Dollars!!* With a little bit of patience and a whole lot of love, I could turn that bargain into something special. After a sexy slow braise that tough cut was packed with flavor and more tender than a mother's love. Grocery Outlet let me flex my creativity without flexing my wallet. But it wasn't just about saving money. It was about having fun. I got to experiment and turn humble ingredients into comfort food where you could taste the love. It gave me the freedom to mess around, try things, and cook with heart, even when we were scraping by.

In 2016, my wife and I made the move to Vallejo—the city we now proudly call home. Even before we officially landed, we were spending weekdays and weekends house hunting and getting a feel for the area. During one of those early trips, we stopped into Seafood City, a market that straight up changed my life. I'd never seen so much fresh seafood in one place—live crab, clams, fish still staring at you. But it wasn't just the seafood. It was the meats. Beef, pork, chicken, rabbit, lamb, goat, off-cuts, and organ meats I'd never seen in a mainstream grocery store. And the aisles were stacked high with every instant noodle you could imagine. It was heaven for a carb-loving fat kid like myself. It was a cook's playground. I walked through those aisles with my mouth watering and my imagination going wild. I left that day with a full cart and a fire lit under me. From pork ears to marinated rabbit to goat stew, I started cooking with new ingredients, learning new flavors, and gaining a deeper appreciation for the Filipino, Vietnamese, and other Asian cultures that make up so much of Vallejo. That market wasn't just a place to shop, it was an education, an inspiration, and one of the reasons I fell so hard for this city. It reminded me that there's always more to learn, more to taste, and more ways to connect through food. That Christmas, in December of 2016, my brother Joe got me a gift that would unknowingly change the entire trajectory of my life: a Weber Smokey Mountain. I hadn't asked for it. In fact, I'd never even used a smoker before, let alone owned one. I sure as hell didn't know how to use it. The only smoking I did was Cali Green. But somehow, he just knew. I remember holding that box and thinking, *"Alright... I guess we're doing this."* A couple days later, I set it up in the backyard, cracked a beer, lit some Kingsford charcoal, tossed in chunks of applewood I picked up from Home Depot, and stood there watching the smoke roll out like it was the opening act to the rest of my life. My first cook was a rack of lamb I picked up from Safeway. I seasoned it, laid it on the grate, closed the lid, and waited. After two beers and a joint, or roughly an hour, I popped the lid open and, I swear to God, I heard music. That lamb had a crust like I'd never seen, the fat was perfectly rendered, and when I sliced into it, it was *Pretty in Pink* Molly Ringwald status, from coast to coast with no gray band in sight. Juicy. Smoky. Gorgeous. That first bite was unlike anything I'd ever cooked. My world changed. It was like my first kiss, the first time I heard Andre Nickatina, and the first time I watched *Showgirls*, all rolled into one. I didn't just taste food, I tasted possibilities. That moment flipped a switch. From that point on, I was obsessed. The fire. The flavor. The therapy of tending a pit. I was hooked.

From then on, I was smoking meats and slappin' beats whenever I could. It was fun, it was therapeutic, it was tasty . . . it was everything I wanted. And I wasn't just cooking, I was *studying*. Watching videos, reading posts, trying new methods, failing, learning, doing it again. I started posting photos of my cooks on an Instagram account I barely used, just to track my own progress. But then, something unexpected happened. I found a community. I started connecting with folks like ThisJewCanQue, Code3Spides, GrillinWithDad, BaconRaiderBBQ, KendrickBBQ, GroarkBoysBBQ, MapleLeafSmokehouse, CanuckSmoker—backyard pitmasters, weekend warriors, pros, and passionate home cooks from all over the place. People who loved this life like I did. "Big John is following me back!" I'd yell to my wife. "Grillin With Dad just hit 20K!" Or "Holy sh*t, Caribeque reposted me!" These weren't just online names, they were my tribe. Then one day, a family friend asked, "Do you cater? I see your Instagram posts, and your food looks amazing." I said, "Yes, of course!" Even though I'd never cooked for anyone outside of family and had zero catering equipment. No warmers, no trays, not even a folding table. But YOLO, right? I figured it out. A few weeks later, I was posted up in Napa, dishing out two briskets, baked beans, macaroni salad, and a fruit tray to a party of fifty-plus. And guess what? They *loved it*. That led to another gig. Then another. Before I knew it, I was cooking, catering, and building something real.

Then came 2020 and everything changed. The world shut down, restaurants closed, and for a minute, everything felt upside down. I don't want to romanticize it, because it was a brutal time for so many, but in the middle of all that chaos, something started to shift for me. With everyone stuck at home, people were scrolling more, craving comfort, craving

connection, and craving good food. My friends kept bugging me to download TikTok. And being a strong man who easily resists peer pressure, I caved and downloaded it. I started posting old clips of my cooks and narrating over them. Nothing fancy or out of the box, just me being me. I'd say, "It cuts like butta" when cutting a steak. I'd yell, "Bang bang Flavorgang" at the end of my videos as a thank you to my followers and an ode the San Francisco 49ers. I'd blurp out, "Official like a ref with a whistle" after tasting my food. It was raw, real, and, despite what many think about my ad libs, completely unscripted. I changed my name from "c_train707" to "ChucksFlavorTrain". Then something about it hit. I woke up one morning with twenty thousand followers . . . then twenty-five thousand . . . then a hundred thousand . . . and before I knew it, I had over a million. And while the world was locked down, people started reaching out. From locals to tourists to tech execs and everyone in-between, asking if I could cater private dinners, since restaurants were closed. I didn't care if you were from across the street or across the country. If you wanted to eat, I wanted to cook for you. That year flipped the switch. What started as a way to pass the time turned into a full-blown calling.

Over the next few years, the ride got wild. I was doing shit I never would have dreamed of. Gordon Ramsay duetted a couple of my TikToks . . . *and gave me props*! He's known for shittin' on folks and hurling insults, but not on my videos. He showed me love. Twice. I got to private chef for a Golden State Warrior, cook for multiple groups of 49ers players and various sports radio personalities. And then, in 2023, I got the call. It was *the* call . . . but it was one I didn't even know I'd been waiting for: *BBQ Brawl*. Season 4. Food Network. I packed up my knives, kissed my wife and daughter goodbye, and went in ready to pour my soul into the experience. It was wild. It was exhausting. It was one of the hardest and most rewarding experiences of my life. It tested me mentally, physically, emotionally. . . . In the end I had nothing left to give. I made it to the finals and that's where my journey ended. But I hadn't lost. I was on national TV for ten weeks, going toe to toe with some of the best pitmasters and chefs in the game. Getting free promotion and exposure. I made friends for life. And to this day, people still approach me in public and say: "You should've won." "You were the people's champ." "Chuck got robbed!" And that's something that chokes me up. Something I can't describe. For a guy who gets drunk and burns shit in his backyard, to be standing in that spotlight, being *seen*, being *celebrated* . . . it's surreal. It's humbling. And it reminds me why I never stopped showing up.

And then . . . the moment that still doesn't feel real. I got to cook with *Emeril Lagasse*. Yeah. That Emeril. The man who made me want to cook in the first place. The guy I watched religiously as a kid. The wild-eyed, garlic-drunk tornado, yelling "BAM!" as he chucked handfuls of seasoning into a pan like a wizard casting a spell. Emeril wasn't just a chef; he was a force. He made food exciting, theatrical, *fun*. He made a chubby little kid with a Turbo Cooker believe he could be someone. So, when I found myself on set with him, working side by side, it was like walking into a dream I didn't even think was possible. He was everything I hoped he'd be, and he left me in awe. Funny, kind, generous with his knowledge, and sharp as ever. He left me starstruck. We cooked, we talked, we laughed, and then we wrapped. That's when I FaceTimed my dad. I tried to play it cool. "Hey, Dad, just checking in. I'm working in New Orleans. Someone wants to say hi." And then I handed the phone to Emeril. And without missing a beat, Emeril jumped into the conversation like they were old fishing buddies. "Hey, Gary, how you doing?!?" My dad casually responded cool as a cucumber. I cried like a baby. Even now as I type this years later, tears are rolling down my cheeks. Because in that moment, watching Emeril talk to my dad, I realized something. I wasn't chasing validation anymore. I had it. I had become the person I used to dream about being while watching Food Network reruns in my parents' living room. It was full circle. From watching Emeril on TV to introducing him to my dad. That moment broke me in a way. It was the first time I truly allowed myself to feel proud. Not for a single recipe or a viral video, but for the whole journey. It was all real. The fat little black kid with a Turbo Cooker and a dream? The one who always felt out of place? The one who struggled with anxiety, depression, and a sense of self-worth? That kid. He made it. *I made it*. I wasn't chasing a dream anymore; I was living it.

Food has brought me joy, community, love, and purpose. It's taken me from Grocery Outlet lamb shanks in a tiny apartment to cooking for NFL players, competing on national TV, and standing next to the legends who inspired me. It's carried me from daytime infomercials to early-morning smokes . . . from backyard hangs with my day ones to BBQ championships with hundreds of thousands watching. And through it all, I've never stopped being that same fat kid with a big appetite, a bigger personality, and an even bigger love for feeding people. Whether I'm smoking ribs in the backyard, throwing down at TFTI's with my day ones, getting wild in the IE with my So Cal fam, or cooking on a sandbar in Key West, I'm still just a big kid having fun. Grilling with my friends, bumpin' Bay Area beats, popping my pinky like a piston, and chasing flavor like it's my full-time job. Because now . . . it is. So, thank you. Whether you've been riding since day one or just hopped on the Flavor Train, I'm glad you're here. Now, let's keep this thang rollin'.

THE CONDUCTOR'S MANIFESTO

My cooking style? Backyard. Down-home. Fun, trust-your-gut cooking. Ain't nothing fancy about it. I once rapped, "Ain't no recipes, a pinch of this, a dash of that," and honestly, that sums it up. It's instinctual. Bold. Messy. And it's mine. I don't measure; I vibe. I taste, adjust, repeat.

If a recipe calls for something I don't like, I swap it. No anchovies? Fish sauce works. Don't like parsley? Boom, cilantro. Unless you're one of those folks who taste soap. Two cloves of garlic? Nah, I'm tossing six. I'm not making food that whispers; I want it to smack you in the mouth. Cooking's not about perfection, it's about flavor and feeling.

If there's one thing I want you to take from this book, it's confidence. Trust your palate. Trust your gut. If it feels off, fix it. If it feels right, lean in. Don't be afraid to toss the rule book in the smoker and see what happens.

When I started smoking meats, I went straight to YouTube University. Everyone's saying the same thing: salt, pepper, garlic, remove the membrane, mustard binder, butcher paper. Technically right, but also kinda bullshit. You think BBQ joints are keeping it that pure? Nah. They're using MSG, seasoned salt, "secret" blends that are really just Lawry's in disguise. I'm not against tradition, but tradition ain't law.

You want flavor? Flip the script. Use a binder that adds something. Fish sauce, soy, or hot sauce all bring extra punch. Want a rich bark that's not rock hard? Wrap it in foil. Don't let the internet BBQ police shame you. Do what works for you.

These "recipes" aren't commandments. They're blueprints, bumpers to keep you in the lane. Most recipes undershoot seasoning. If it tastes flat, add salt. Needs a kick? Bring the heat. Use this book as inspiration, not incarceration. Your taste buds are the GPS.

We're in a food renaissance. Social media made global flavors instant. See something wild? Try it. Google a country and a protein and let the algorithm cook. I've made everything from gator to goat. Maybe gator ain't for you, but that crispy lechon-style pork belly? Fire. Borrow, remix, evolve.

To the "don't change the recipe" crowd, how do we ever create something new? Try it. Fail gloriously. Try again. Cook drunk, cook weird, cook bold. Nobody remembers the measurements; they remember how it tasted. Food isn't perfection, it's connection. So bring the flavor, bring the fun, make it loud, and make it you.

COLLOPACK
SOLUTIONS
weber

weber
Searwood
PIT BARREL
weber

Pre-Travel Checklist

GRILLS VS. SMOKERS: WHAT'S THE DIFFERENCE?

Before we dive into the gear, let's talk about the game. At its core, a grill is a cooking surface over high, direct heat. Think of it as your sprinter: fast, hot, and built for quick cooks like steaks, burgers, and chops. A grill gives you those beautiful char marks and a crispy sear. A smoker is an insulated chamber built for low, indirect heat and fire management. It's your marathon runner: slow, steady, and designed to burn fuel for hours to break down tough cuts like brisket or pork shoulder, turning them into gold using smoke. Understanding this difference is how you decide what gear is right for the cook.

Anatomy of a Grill

Cooking grate: Cast iron retains heat and builds better crust. Stainless steel cleans easier and lasts longer. Chrome-plated is common, but it doesn't hold up over time.

Charcoal grate: Where your fuel burns. In a Kettle, it's adjustable. On a Kamado, it's fixed.

Firebox: For offsets and pellet smokers. This is where the magic begins.

Lid: Holds in convection heat. The dome shape helps circulate smoke and flavor.

Vents and dampers: The real temp controls. Bottom vent = oxygen = more fire. Top vent = heat and smoke out. You control the fire by balancing both.

Ash catcher: Ash blocks airflow, so clean the catcher regularly. Less ash = better combustion = cleaner smoke.

Grease-management system: On gas or pellet grills, you need a drip tray or grease bucket to prevent flare-ups and fires. In an offset smoker, there will likely be a hole that drips grease into a bucket.

TOOLS OF THE TRADE

Basting Brushes and Mops

Basting brushes and mops aren't just for esthetics. They're tools that help you build complexity, moisture, and sheen. Done right, they take your meat from "good backyard BBQ" to "how the hell did you make this?"

WHEN TO USE WHAT:

- **The brush equals control.** Think thick sauces, glazes, or butters applied near the end of the cook. You want precision and a glossy finish.
- **The mop equals moisture and flavor layers.** Use throughout long smokes to keep bark moist and meat juicy. You're not painting. You're flavoring.

TREAT THEM RIGHT—CLEANING AND STORAGE

- **Silicone brushes:** Dishwasher-safe. Rinse and roll.
- **Cotton mops:** Wash with hot soapy water, dry thoroughly. If it starts to smell like an old gym sock, it's time to toss it.
- Store brushes and mops dry, away from your fire tools. They ain't your tongs. They're your flavor applicators.

The right tool, at the right time, makes the difference between a sticky, flavor-blasted bark and a soggy, over-sauced mess. Whether you're layering honey butter on grilled cornbread or mopping a brisket with beer and beef tallow, use the right brush, keep it clean, and know your timing. Sauce control is flavor control. Don't sleep on it.

Spray Bottles

You ever see ribs with that perfect bark? Dark, sticky, glistening like they just came off a commercial shoot? Or brisket that's got that deep mahogany sheen, with just the right amount of shine and texture on the surface? That's not just seasoning and smoke. That's **spritz work**. Spray bottles are the low-key MVP of long cooks. They help control the texture of your bark, keep the surface from drying out, add flavor as you go, and give your meat a just-cooked look that screams "take a bite of me now." It's a small tool with a big impact.

Level up—why you need one:

- **Moisture maintenance:** Long cooks equal dry air, especially on offset pits or in colder weather. Spritzing keeps the meat from drying out and helps you push through the stall without crusting over your bark too early.
- **Bark development:** Smoke loves moisture. Moist meat grabs smoke particles and builds bark faster and better than dry surfaces. The spritz gives smoke something to stick to.
- **Surface cooling:** Spritzing cools the surface of the meat just slightly, helping regulate cooking speed and promoting deeper smoke penetration. It keeps you from cooking too hot, too fast on the outside.
- **Flavor layering:** You're not just spraying water here. You can build flavor into your spritz that subtly seasons every layer of the bark while the meat smokes.

WHAT TO PUT IN IT

Here's where you can start having fun. Think of your spritz as a **light seasoning mist**. It's not gonna soak in deep, but it *will* hit the outer layer every time you spray. So build it like a finishing salt. Simple, but with purpose.

CLASSIC COMBOS:

- **Apple cider vinegar (ACV):** Go-to base. Great for pork, brisket, and ribs. It cuts through fat and adds a gentle tang.
- **Fifty/fifty apple juice and water:** Adds sweetness, promotes caramelization, and helps with bark formation on ribs and pork butts.
- **Beef broth and Worcestershire sauce:** Rich, meaty combo for brisket or beef ribs. Adds umami and keeps the surface dark and juicy.
- **Beer or bourbon:** For the flex. Great on chuck roasts, short ribs, or anything you want to hit with that malty edge.
- **Pickle juice:** IYKYK. Salty, sour, and shockingly good on chicken and pork.

SPRITZ BLENDS:

- **Brisket spritz:** ¾ beef broth, ¼ Worcestershire sauce, splash of ACV
- **Pork spritz:** Equal parts apple juice, water, and ACV
- **Rib glaze pre-game:** Apple cider vinegar plus a dash of honey water
- **Smoky chicken mist:** Pickle brine, lemon juice, tiny splash of hot sauce

Bin the Bristle Brushes

Let's talk facts: Wire bristle grill brushes are a bad idea. I don't care how much the brush cost or what the label says: Those little metal bristles can snap off, stick to your grates, and end up in your food. And if someone takes a bite and swallows one? That's a fast track to the ER. This isn't some urban legend. It's happened to real people. Punctured throats, stomach issues, surgery. All because of a five-dollar brush. So, here's the rule: If your brush sheds, toss it. It's not worth the risk when you've got safer options. Keep your food safe. Keep your people safe. Lose the wires.

Level up:

WHEN TO SPRITZ?

Timing is everything. Go too early and you'll wash off the rub before it sets. Go too late and the bark's already sealed.

- **Start spritzing after 90 minutes to 2 hours:** Let the bark begin to form first. You want it to "set" before adding moisture.
- **Spritz every 45 to 60 minutes after that:** Enough to keep the surface moist, not so much that you're steaming your meat. Light mist, not a garden hose.
- **Stop spritzing once you wrap:** Whether you wrap in foil or butcher paper, you've moved into the finishing zone. No more open spritzing from here on out.

WHAT KIND OF BOTTLE?

Not all bottles are created equal. You want one that sprays evenly, doesn't clog, and can handle acidic liquids without corroding or leaking. These are my must-haves when looking for a spray bottle:

- Food-safe plastic (PET or HDPE)
- Adjustable spray head for fine mist or stream control
- Easy to clean and refill
- **Dedicated to BBQ only:** Don't reuse your old Windex bottle. We're making bark, not bleaching brisket.

HOW DO I SPRITZ LIKE A PRO?

- **Warm your spritz:** Spraying cold liquid on hot meat cools the surface too much and can shock the bark. Let your spritz sit out while your fire warms up.
- **Don't over-spritz:** Too much moisture breaks down the bark and can turn it soggy. Keep it light and consistent.
- **Label your bottles:** You don't want to reach for beef broth and accidentally hit your ribs with bourbon vinegar. Or maybe you do, but you should know which one is which.
- **Use colored bottles:** Or painter's tape to mark flavor profiles. Red cap for ribs. Green cap for brisket. Blue for poultry. Keep it organized, keep it flavorful.

The spray bottle might not be flashy, but it's a bark-building beast and a pro-level move that separates casual grillers from folks who really know what they're doing. You're not just keeping meat moist, you're setting up smoke to stick, bark to shine, and flavor to stack. So, fill it up, keep it close, and give your BBQ the mist it deserves.

Cutting Boards

You spent all day tending the fire. You seasoned that meat like a boss. You built bark, dialed in the temps, hit the stall, wrapped, rested . . . and now it's go time. The slice. The shred. The serve. And let me tell you right now, this is where a lot of folks fumble. The final phase of the cook is just as important as the first. That means you need the right setup. The right board, the right knife, the right mind-set. Treat your meat with the same respect off the grill as you did on it.

THE CUTTING BOARD

Let's start here. This isn't just a place to slice. It's your carving station. Your juice catcher. Your final flavor zone. If you've got a board that's slippery and too small or lacking a juice groove, you're in for a messy surprise. Here are some things to look for in a board:

- **Big surface area:** You're not slicing strawberries. You need a board that can hold a full brisket, a pork butt, or a few racks of ribs without meat falling off the sides.
- **Juice groove:** Crucial. When you slice into a juicy cut, it's gonna run. A groove catches the drippings and saves your counter from becoming a crime scene.
- **Non-slip base:** Whether it's rubber feet or a wet towel underneath, your board should stay put while you're carving. A sliding board is how knives end up where they shouldn't.

MATERIAL MATTERS

- **Wood or composite:** End-grain butcher block is king. It's gentle on knives and looks sexy in photos. Plastic is fine for raw meat prep (avoid cutting on it), but wood is the real MVP for presentation and final slicing.
- **Avoid glass or stone:** Looks fancy, destroys your knives. Leave that in the kitchen showroom.

Knives

Let's get into knives. Unlike most of the gear we've covered, this is where you can show a little personality. Your knife can be as loud or as low-key as you want. You want something that looks like it came out of a samurai dojo? Go for it. Prefer a no-frills twenty-five-dollar Victorinox that gets the job done every time? That's a win too. I don't care what it costs, I care that it holds an edge, fits comfortably in your hand, and doesn't try to murder your brisket (or your fingers). I've got knives that cost less than lunch, and some that cost more than rent. Doesn't matter. What matters is that you treat them right, use them right, and keep them sharp. Because here's the truth: A dull blade is the most dangerous thing in your kitchen. It'll slip, it'll shred, and it'll make a mess of everything you worked for. All that tenderness you built? Gone in two seconds if you're sawing through it with some clunky gas-station blade. So, if you're constantly sharpening every few weeks just to keep your knife functional? It's time to toss it and upgrade.

KNIFE ESSENTIALS

Here's what you really need: nothing crazy, just a few solid blades that cover all your BBQ needs.

Carving knife or slicing knife: Long, narrow, and smooth-edged. Not serrated. This is your brisket weapon. You want clean, even cuts that glide through bark and fat like butter, not torn meat that looks like it got run over.

Boning knife: Thin, flexible, razor-sharp. Perfect for trimming fat caps, separating ribs, deboning poultry, or any kind of prep work where finesse matters more than brute force.

Chef's knife: This is your daily driver. Use it for chopping herbs, slicing onions, prepping rub ingredients, or smashing garlic. A good chef's knife stays in your hand all day.

Meat cleaver (optional): If you're doing whole hog, goat, lamb, or anything that needs bone-splitting power, a cleaver is clutch. Otherwise, it's a nice-to-have tool that looks badass on the wall.

Level up: Knives aren't just sharp sticks. They're the finishing move. They're what turns smoked meat into something beautiful. Invest in a few good ones, keep 'em clean, keep 'em sharp, and they'll take care of you for years to come.

Keep it sharp. Run a honing rod over the blade after every few uses. If it starts dragging through a tomato, it's time for a real sharpening.

Use the right knife for the right job. Don't carve brisket with a paring knife or try to fillet fish with a cleaver. Respect the tools.

Grip matters. A knife should feel locked in, balanced, and comfortable in your hand. If it feels flimsy or awkward, it's gonna be trouble.

Brands I trust? Start with Wüsthof, Messermeister, Zwilling, or Victorinox. Solid steel, consistent quality, and they won't fail you in the middle of a big cook.

Resting Trays and Drip Management

Before you even touch a knife, you've got to rest your meat. This step is sacred. What you'll need:

- **Stainless steel tray or sheet pan:** Use it to catch the meat as it comes off the smoker. Line it with butcher paper or foil to keep it clean and easy.
- **Resting rack:** Place the meat on a wire rack over the tray so it doesn't stew in its own juices. This keeps the bark crisp while letting it rest evenly.
- **Towels, cambro, or cooler** (for big cuts)**:** Wrap large cuts like brisket or pork shoulder in butcher paper or foil, then tuck them into a cooler lined with towels or a cambro. Rest for 1 to 2 hours minimum, or 8 to 12 hours if you want to go pro-level. It's not just about temperature; it's about juice redistribution.

Level up: That post-cook rest is where the magic happens. Don't slice too early unless you like dry meat and regret.

Final Word: Respect Your Tools

Your grill might be the beast, but these tools are how you tame it. If you're fumbling with junky tongs, poking steaks instead of temping them, or guessing when your ribs are done, you're not giving the meat the respect it deserves. Invest in good gear. Take care of it. Learn how to use it like a craftsman. Because when you've got the right tools in your hands, you're not just cooking, you're commanding the fire.

THE SPICE RACK

Flavor starts here. Your pantry should be built like a linebacker: versatile, powerful, and always ready.

Spices and Seasonings

- Kosher salt, freshly ground black pepper
- Garlic and onion powder (go granulated, when possible)
- Smoked paprika, ground cumin, mustard powder, chili powder
- Heat: cayenne, Aleppo, chipotle peppers
- Complexity: celery seed, allspice, coriander
- MSG: Use it. That's flavor insurance.

Oils

- High smoke point: avocado, canola, grapeseed
- EVOO: Use for marinades, chimichurri, finishing
- Neutral: grapeseed, vegetable, canola, sunflower

Sauces and condiments

- Ketchup, mustard, ACV, Worcestershire sauce
- Soy sauce, hot sauce (get a collection)
- Honey, maple syrup, molasses
- Mayo: Alabama White Sauce (page 35) base. Don't knock it.

BARBEQUE
LEMON STEPPER
PREMIUM QUALITY
EST.
THE MVP
"SO GOOD IT SHOULD BE ILLEGAL"
BOARS NIGHT OUT
WHITE LIGHTNING
WITH
DOUBLE GARLIC BUTTER
SEASONING FOR BEEF, PORK, CHICKEN, VEGGIES & FISH
NET WT 12.2 oz (346g)
THE USUAL
ALL PURPOSE
FIRE & SMOKE
SOCIETY
Meat Mitch
CANDIED JALAPEÑO
SEASONING & RUB
Net Weight 12.5oz (354g)
BBQ RUB
WT 10.5 oz (298g)
CAJUN
HONEY RUB
NET WT 11 oz (312 G)
KENWOOD'S
KRB
RUSTIC BLENDS
SIGNATURE RUB
COMPETITION BLEND
NET WT. 12.5OZ (354G)
GRILLIN WITH DAD
DAD'S TACO SEASONING
Perfect on Chicken, Pork, Beef and Veggies
Net Wt. 9.7 oz (275g)
WORLD CHAMPION
Loot N' Booty BBQ
EVERYTHING RUB
NET WT 14 OZ (397 G)

SPICY STEAK RUB
RUBCITY ROARK BOYS BBQ Pork
NET WT. 6.17 OZ (175 g)
Guy Fieri's FLAVORTOWN
ULTIMATE STEAK BUTTER RUB
THE MVP
RUBCITY GROARK BOYS BBQ Beef
NET WT. 6.17 OZ (175 g)
Guy Fieri's FLAVORTOWN
GARLIC BUTTER ALL PURPOSE RUB
MADE - IN - TEXAS
GABRICK BARBECUE
ALL PURPOSE RUB SEASONING
NET WT 9.8 OZ (277.82g)
MEAT DAVE
ALL PURPOSE SEASONING & RUB
LANE'S BETHLEHEM, GA
STEAK SUPREME
www.LANESBBQ.com
LANE'S BETHLEHEM, GA
big dill PICKLE BRINE
GLUTEN FREE
www.LANESBBQ.com
PREMIUM
HARDCORE CARNIVORE
Cowboy Butter Mix
TO MAKE YOUR OWN Just Add BUTTER INSTANT COMPOUND
HARD CORE CARNIVORE
B·L·A·C·K
BEEF SEASONING
NET WEIGHT 13.00 OZ (368 G)
HARDCORE CARNIVORE
Hot Honey Butter Mix
TO MAKE YOUR OWN Just Add BUTTER INSTANT COMPOUND
NET WEIGHT 12.50 oz (354g)
Nutrition Facts
JESS PRYLES
CARNIVORE
AMPLIFY
MEGA SAVORY FLAVOR DUST
DEREK WOLF APPROVED

Rubs

Seasoning is more than just salt and pepper. It's the soul of your food. The bass line in your BBQ symphony. The thing that makes people stop mid-bite and say, "What the hell is in this, and why do I want to drink it?" Some folks are purists. Salt, pepper, garlic, and smoke. That's it. Others have spice blends that have been passed down like treasure maps, hidden behind the turmeric no one's used since 2008. Either way, the point is the same: Flavor is king. I don't care if you're rocking a twenty-dollar artisan rub or something you picked up next to the register at the gas station. If you use it right, it'll work.

When I first started out, I wasn't making my own rubs. I bought whatever had a cool label or decent reviews. And to be honest? I still do. Probably 60 percent of the time I'm grabbing something off the shelf or online. Why? Because it's easy, and, honestly, some of these brands are crushing it. But once you learn how to make your own, the real fun begins. You can tweak it to be spicier, saltier, tangier, or sugar-free if you're feeling virtuous. Love a store-bought blend but wish it didn't taste like candy? Adjust it. Some of my favorite brands are Kosmos Q, Heath Riles BBQ, and Blazing Star BBQ. But that's just me. Making your own rubs turns your spice cabinet into a playground. You become the mixologist of meat. The Willy Wonka of umami. Only instead of chocolate rivers, you've got brisket juice and a countertop covered in paprika.

There are a few lesser-known ingredients I like to use. Sumac brings this bright, citrusy zip that cuts through rich meats like a chainsaw through butter. Aleppo pepper is earthy, sweet, and just hot enough to remind you it's in the room. And, yes, I use MSG. Calm down. It's not evil. It's delicious. If your food makes someone close their eyes and say, "Damn," there's probably MSG, butter, or salt involved. Usually, all three.

Let's start with some basic rubs. These are the ones I keep in the bull pen, ready to go. Tweak them. Remix them. Sub ingredients like you're swapping players in a fantasy draft. I'm not precious about it and you shouldn't be either.

AP BBQ Rub

YIELD: ABOUT ½ CUP

¼ cup packed light brown sugar
1 tablespoon kosher salt
1 tablespoon freshly ground black pepper
1 tablespoon garlic powder
1 tablespoon onion powder
1 teaspoon mustard powder
1 teaspoon paprika
½ teaspoon cayenne pepper or Aleppo pepper, for a unique twist (optional)

This all-purpose BBQ rub is perfect for anything. Feel free to adjust the ratios to suit your taste.

HOW TO MAKE IT: Combine all the ingredients in a bowl and mix thoroughly. Store in an airtight container in a cool, dark, and dry place for up to 6 months.

SPG+ Rub

YIELD: ¾ CUP

¼ cup kosher salt
¼ cup freshly ground black pepper
2 tablespoons granulated garlic
1 tablespoon granulated onion
1 teaspoon celery seed
1 teaspoon MSG (do it, trust me)

This "salt, pepper, garlic, and some other stuff" rub goes great on everything.

HOW TO MAKE IT: Mix all the ingredients together in a bowl until well combined. Keep in an airtight container and it will last for up to a year.

Coffee Rub

YIELD: ABOUT ½ CUP

1 tablespoon instant coffee

¼ cup packed light brown sugar

2 tablespoons kosher salt

2 tablespoons sumac

2 tablespoons granulated garlic

2 teaspoons freshly ground black pepper

1 teaspoon allspice

1 teaspoon cocoa powder

This rub is guaranteed to wake up your beef and chicken.

HOW TO MAKE IT: Combine all the ingredients in a bowl and mix until everything is evenly distributed. Store in an airtight container in a cool, dark, and dry place for up to 6 months.

Lemon Pepper Herb Rub

YIELD: ABOUT ⅓ CUP

2 tablespoons lemon pepper

1 tablespoon dried thyme

1 tablespoon dried oregano

1 tablespoon granulated garlic

½ tablespoon kosher salt (adjust based on the salt level of your lemon pepper)

½ tablespoon freshly ground black pepper

1 teaspoon ground sumac (optional, but trust me)

This rub is fantastic on seafood or chicken . . . it's truly addicting.

HOW TO MAKE IT: Mix all the ingredients in a bowl until fully blended. Store in an airtight container in a cool, dark, and dry place for up to 6 months.

Sweet Heat Island Rub

YIELD: ⅓ CUP

¼ cup packed light brown sugar

1 tablespoon kosher salt

1 tablespoon garlic powder

1 teaspoon allspice

1 teaspoon Aleppo pepper or red pepper flakes

½ teaspoon paprika

½ teaspoon ground cinnamon

½ teaspoon grated nutmeg

Pork loves this one, and chicken does too! Try it on seafood if you're really feelin' wild!

HOW TO MAKE IT: Combine all the ingredients in a bowl and mix thoroughly. Keep in an airtight container in a cool, dark, and dry place for up to 6 months.

TENAYO
ROASTED POBLANO
MEXICAN-STYLE BARBECUE SAUCE
SMOKY & EARTHY
NET WT. 14.5 OZ (411g)
TENAYO
MOLE ROJO
MEXICAN-STYLE BARBECUE SAUCE
PEPPERY & BRIGHT
NET WT. 13.5 OZ (383g)
KENWOOD'S KRB RUSTIC BLENDS
CHIPOTLE SAUCE
SMOKY WITH A SPICY KICK
HEAT MEDIUM
BOLD FLAVOR
NET WT. 12 FL OZ (355ML)
MELINDA'S
SWEET & SPICY
JAPANESE BARBECUE SAUCE
MADE WITH NATURAL INGREDIENTS
DRUNK CHICKS CRAFT SAUCES
EST. 2020
SWEET SIRACHA HOT SAUCE
Net 12 fl. Oz. (355ml)
DOWN RIGHT DELICIOUS
DREW'S DRIZZLE
BBQ SAUCE
NET WT 18 oz (1 LB. 2 OZ) (0.51 kg)
BEAR & BURTON'S
Breakfast Sauce too
So good you'll want breakfast all day!
BEAR & BURTON'S
SMALL BATCH
W Sauce
AMERICA'S WORCESTERSHIRE

MELINDA'S
ORIGINAL HABANERO
MANGO
PEPPER SAUCE
Net Wt. 10 fl. oz. (296mL)
MELINDA'S
CREAMY STYLE
GHOST PEPPER
WING SAUCE
AND CONDIMENT
Net Wt. 12 fl. oz. (355mL)
MELINDA'S
BLACK
TRUFFLE
HOT SAUCE
Net Wt. 12 fl. oz. (355mL)
FYR
PROVISIONS
TIKI
TIKI
BBQ SAUCE
PINEAPPLE
SOY SAUCE
RED CHILES
NET WT 13.5 OZ (400 ml)
FYR
PROVISIONS
TIKI
TIKI
BBQ SAUCE
PINEAPPLE
SOY SAUCE
RED CHILES
BEAR & BURTON'S
SMALL BATCH
W Sauce
NATURALLY GLUTEN FREE
FIRESHIRE
Net 12 FL OZ (355mL)
BEAR & BURTON'S
Breakfast Sauce
NATURALLY GLUTEN FREE
A Little Sweet
A Little Heat
BEAR & BURTON'S
SMALL BATCH
W Sauce
NATURALLY GLUTEN FREE
AMERICA'S
WORCESTERSHIRE
BEAR & BURTON'S
SMALL
W Sauce
FIRESHIRE

Sauces

Now let's talk about sauces. Rubs build the foundation, but sauce? Sauce is the top coat. The final flourish. The little black dress that turns Tuesday-night chicken thighs into something you'd serve to guests. I always recommend having three kinds of sauces in your arsenal: a good, bold BBQ sauce, something tangy or mustardy, and a fresh herb-based one that doesn't need cooking. That way, you've got something for any flavor combo you throw on the grill. Store-bought sauces are fine. Great, even. I keep bottles from Five Monkeys, Heath Riles, and Blazing Star on standby. And if I'm stuck at a gas station in the middle of nowhere? Sweet Baby Ray's to the rescue. But making your own is surprisingly easy. You control the sugar, the salt, and the vibe. No mystery goo. No nineteen-syllable preservatives. Just flavor. Here are five to get you started. Keep them simple, tweak them if you want, and don't worry about being fancy. These are workhorses, not show ponies.

Sweet and Smoky BBQ Sauce

YIELD: 1½ CUPS

1 cup ketchup

¼ cup apple cider vinegar

¼ cup packed light brown sugar

2 tablespoons honey (use maple syrup or molasses for a different flavor)

1 tablespoon Worcestershire sauce

1 tablespoon garlic powder

½ tablespoon onion powder

1 teaspoon smoked paprika

Kosher salt and freshly ground black pepper

This is the BBQ sauce everyone will love.

HOW TO MAKE IT: Combine all ingredients in a saucepan, seasoning to taste with salt and pepper. Bring to a simmer over medium heat, then reduce the heat to low and cook for 15 to 20 minutes, stirring occasionally, until the sauce thickens to your liking. Taste and adjust the seasonings as needed. Can be stored in the refrigerator for up to 3 weeks in an airtight container.

Cali Gold Sauce

YIELD: 1½ CUPS

1 cup yellow mustard

½ cup apple cider vinegar

¼ cup packed light brown sugar

2 tablespoons honey

2 tablespoons garlic powder

1 tablespoon Worcestershire sauce

A couple dashes of hot sauce (use your favorite and add to taste)

This tangy and vibrant sauce is great on pork, chicken, and sausages.

HOW TO MAKE IT: Whisk all the ingredients together in a bowl until smooth. For best flavor, let it sit in the refrigerator for at least 30 minutes before serving. Can be stored for 2 to 3 days in an airtight container.

Alabama White Sauce

YIELD: 1¼ CUPS

1 cup mayonnaise

¼ cup apple cider vinegar

1 tablespoon Worcestershire sauce

1 tablespoon prepared horseradish

½ tablespoon minced garlic, or 1 teaspoon garlic powder

½ teaspoon freshly ground black pepper

Freshly squeezed lemon juice

Kosher salt

This sauce is a flavor powerhouse—tangy, fresh, and creamy. It's fantastic on chicken, pork, and seafood.

HOW TO MAKE IT: In a bowl, whisk together all the ingredients until smooth and well combined seasoning to taste with lemon juice and salt. Taste and adjust with lemon juice and salt as needed. Chill for at least 30 minutes before serving to allow the flavors to meld. Store in the refrigerator for up to 7 days.

Chimichurri

YIELD: 1 CUP

½ cup finely chopped fresh flat-leaf parsley

½ cup finely chopped fresh cilantro

5 cloves garlic, minced

1 teaspoon dried oregano

½ teaspoon red pepper flakes

½ cup extra-virgin olive oil

2 tablespoons red wine vinegar

1 tablespoon freshly squeezed lemon juice

Kosher salt and freshly ground black pepper

This sauce is so good, it's almost like a cheat code.

HOW TO MAKE IT: In a bowl, combine the parsley, cilantro, garlic, oregano, and red pepper flakes. Stir in the olive oil, red wine vinegar, and lemon juice. Season with salt and pepper to taste. Let the mixture sit for at least 15 minutes before serving to allow the flavors to develop. Can be stored for 2 to 3 days in an airtight container

Mango Habanero Glaze

YIELD: 1¼ CUPS

1 cup mango nectar or pureed mango

1 habanero pepper, seeded and minced

2 tablespoons honey

1 tablespoon freshly squeezed lime juice

1 tablespoon BBQ rub of choice

Pinch of kosher salt

I made this for the first time ever on national TV, and I've been making it ever since. The judges loved it, and I hope you will too!

HOW TO MAKE IT: Combine all the ingredients in a small saucepan. Bring to a gentle simmer over medium heat, then reduce the heat to low and cook for 10 to 15 minutes, stirring occasionally, until the glaze thickens slightly. Be careful not to let it get too thick. Let the glaze cool before using. Can be stored in the refrigerator for up to 3 weeks in an airtight container.

The MVPs

Last but not least, let's give a slow clap to the real MVPs in my fridge: fish sauce, soy sauce, and Worcestershire sauce. These three are flavor grenades. Just a splash can turn a flat sauce or stew into something deep, savory, and borderline addictive. You'll see them all over this book. And even if you don't, feel free to sneak them in anyway. Trust your gut.

At the end of the day, flavor is where the magic lives. Don't let food snobs ruin it for you. If it tastes good, it is good. Keep things simple, season with confidence, and always taste as you go. You'll know when you hit the sweet spot. And if you go too far? That's what beer and napkins are for. Covered, smothered, and flavor-packed. That's the way we roll.

THE PREP DECK

Let's get one thing straight right out of the gate. Great BBQ doesn't start when you light the fire. It doesn't start when the smoke rolls in or when the meat hits the grate. It starts way before all that. I'm talking about the quiet stuff. The behind-the-scenes moments. The trimming, the salting, the mixing, the organizing. The boring-but-beautiful parts nobody talks about because they're too busy showing off the final cut like it came out of nowhere. But here's the thing. That big, juicy, crusty, melt-in-your-mouth brisket? It didn't just happen. It was earned. In the fridge. On the cutting board. During the prep. If the pit is your concert, prep is band practice. If BBQ is a heist, prep is where you draw up the plan and figure out who's driving the getaway car. You can wing it if you want, but you'll be serving chaos on a platter.

Let's talk about salt. It's not fancy. It's not new. It's not even all that exciting on its own. But salt is the secret handshake of good BBQ. It's the start of the flavor party and the reason your meat tastes like something instead of sadness. Dry brining is exactly what it sounds like. You take kosher salt and you season your meat ahead of time. That's it. No brine buckets. No weird science. Just salt and time. And it works. The salt pulls out moisture from the meat, mixes with those juices, and then gets pulled back in. While it's in there, it seasons the meat all the way through and helps it stay juicy when it hits the heat. If you've ever had chicken that tastes like something besides air, thank salt. Big cuts like brisket, pork shoulder, bone-in chicken? These are your dry-brine MVPs. They benefit the most from that salty head start. Give it at least an hour but overnight is where the magic really happens. And leave it uncovered in the fridge if you can. That dries out the surface a bit, so you get that deep, golden crust instead of a steamed meat sweater. Bonus move: If you've got multiple meats in the fridge, label them. Nothing like opening the door and wondering, "Wait, is this pork shoulder or the chuck roast?" at seven a.m. with sleep still in your eyes.

Now, the trimming. Yeah, I know. Not the sexiest part of BBQ. But look, not all fat is your friend. Some of it melts into your meat like liquid gold. Some of it just sits there and turns into a rubbery disaster that ruins the bite. So, you gotta know what to keep and what to kick to the curb. Brisket's a perfect example. You want to trim that fat cap down to about a quarter inch. Round off the edges so you don't end up with burnt corners that taste like charcoal. And absolutely get rid of that silver skin on the underside. That stuff doesn't break down, doesn't take on rub, and basically acts like armor against everything you're trying to do. Ribs? Cut off the flap meat and grill it up. Square up any dangling ends and remove any mangled ribs. Chicken's got its own problems. Excess skin and big globs of fat can lead to flare-ups and soggy bites. Trim it down so you get even cooking and crispy skin instead of a grease fire that sends your eyebrows into early retirement. And, please, get yourself a sharp boning knife. A dull blade will have you hacking away like a caveman and cursing every five seconds. A good knife makes the whole process cleaner, faster, and a lot more fun.

If you're low on time or just wanna bring a different kind of flavor to the party, marinades are where it's at. They're fast, they're flexible, and they're kinda like spa day for your meat. A little acid, a little oil, a handful of bold herbs and spices, and boom!!! Your boring chicken thigh just graduated from community college and got a promotion. Marinades are perfect for thinner cuts. Think chicken thighs, pork chops, skirt steak. Let them soak for 30 minutes to a couple hours and they'll come out tasting like you knew what you were doing all along. Now, don't get carried away with the acid. You go too hard or too long and you'll end up with meat that feels like it's halfway to ceviche. Acid breaks stuff down, which is good in moderation. Too much and your texture goes weird. Pro move? Set aside a little marinade before the meat goes in. Reduce it down later and use it as a glaze. That drizzle on top at the end? That's what makes people lean back in their chairs and say, "Damn."

When you've got time to plan ahead, nothing beats a dry rub. This is where you get to build layers. Flavor on flavor. Texture. Bark. That big, dramatic, mahogany crust that makes people take photos before they take bites. Cover your meat generously. Let it sit at least an hour. Longer if you can. Overnight is the sweet spot. That extra time gives your rub a chance to work its way in and marry up with the meat. I like to make my rubs in batches and keep them in sealed jars. That way I'm not digging around with porky fingers looking for garlic powder like I'm on a scavenger hunt. Label your rubs too. A jar that just says "SPICY" is not helpful when you're mid-cook and trying to remember if that's for chicken or beef.

Mise en place. I know, I know, it sounds like the name of a fancy brunch spot, but it's really just a French way of saying, "Don't be a slob." It means having everything in its place before you start cooking. And it's how you avoid that frantic, sweaty panic that happens when you realize your tongs are on the other side of the yard and your cutting board's under a bag of charcoal. Lay out your trays. One for raw meat. One for prepped. One for finished. Set up your gloves, paper towels, knives, thermometer, foil, your drink of choice, and whatever else you rely on to stay sane. Keep backups of everything because, trust me, you'll lose something mid-cook and having an extra pair of tongs might just save your whole vibe. Chop your aromatics, portion your sauces, get your tools where they need to be. If you've ever tried to season meat with one greasy hand while unscrewing a spice jar with the other, you already know why this step matters.

Once you've got your prep dialed in, take five minutes to plan your cook. If your ribs are gonna ride for five hours, don't just stand there watching them sweat. Use that time. Prep your sides. Get tomorrow's protein ready. Clean up. Organize. Rest. You don't need a military operation here, just a little intention. Jot down a few notes. Use your phone. Make a checklist. You'd be surprised how much smoother things go when you're not winging it like it's BBQ amateur hour.

Prep doesn't get the spotlight. Nobody's writing love songs about trimming fat and labeling spice jars. But this is where you win. This is where you build confidence. This is where you shift from guessing to knowing, from hoping to *hell yes*. Trim it right. Salt it smart. Season with purpose. Stay organized. You're not just cooking. You're setting yourself up to cruise. When it's time to hit the pit, you're not scrambling. You're flowing. You're locked in. You're driving the Flavor Train. And that sucker doesn't run on chaos. So, sharpen that knife. Fire up that playlist. Crack something cold. The whistle's blowin' and it's full steam ahead.

Let's ride.

CHAPTER 1

BEEF
THE CATTLE CAR

The Cattle Car is loaded up with beef in all its juicy, smoky, tender glory. If it ever mooed, we're cookin' it. Brisket that falls apart like plans you didn't want to make anyway. Smashburgers that bring the heat. Tri-tip that hits harder than Patrick Willis in his prime. This chapter's all gas and no brakes. You'll find bold, beefy recipes that go from backyard classics to wild flavor rides. We're talking ribs, roasts, stews, steaks, and a few surprises you probably didn't see coming. Some dishes are fast, some take time, and they're all delicious. Let's get beefy.

Bang Bang, FLAVORGANG!

Tri-Tip with Asian Chimichurri

Tri-Tip is a staple here out West. Don't get me wrong, there's nothing wrong with a classic SPG seasoned one. But my version here is amplified, kicked up, and flavor-packed. Smoked, seared to build a luscious crust, and served with an Asian-inspired chimichurri that packs a serious flavor punch. This is the East meets West BBQ mashup you didn't know you needed.

SERVES: 4 TO 6
PREP TIME: 15 MINUTES
COOK TIME: 1 HOUR 20 MINUTES
REST TIME: 15 TO 20 MINUTES

TRI-TIP

1 tablespoon kosher salt

1 tablespoon freshly ground black pepper

2 teaspoons granulated garlic

One 2½-to-3-pound tri-tip roast

ASIAN CHIMICHURRI

¾ cup finely chopped fresh flat-leaf parsley

1 cup finely chopped fresh cilantro

2 green onions, green parts only, thinly sliced

3 cloves garlic, minced

1 tablespoon finely grated fresh ginger

2 teaspoons sriracha

2 tablespoons fish sauce

2 tablespoons soy sauce

¼ cup rice vinegar

1 tablespoon toasted sesame oil

½ cup neutral oil (such as grapeseed or avocado oil)

½ tablespoon light brown sugar

Freshly ground black pepper

PREPARE THE TRI-TIP: Preheat your smoker to 250°F. In a small bowl, mix the salt, pepper, and garlic. Season the tri-tip evenly with about 2 tablespoons of the seasoning blend. Place the tri-tip in the smoker and cook until the internal temperature reaches 120°F, about 1 hour.

MAKE THE ASIAN CHIMICHURRI: While the tri-tip smokes, combine all the chimichurri ingredients, with pepper to taste, in a bowl. Stir well and adjust the seasoning to taste. Let it sit at room temperature while the tri-tip finishes cooking—the flavors will deepen.

FINAL SEAR AND SERVE: When the tri-tip hits 120°F, remove it from the smoker. Preheat a cast-iron skillet or charcoal grill to high heat. Sear the tri-tip, flipping every 30 to 45 seconds for 5 to 7 minutes, until a crust forms and the internal temp hits 125°F to 130°F for medium rare. Rest the tri-tip for 15 to 20 minutes, then slice it against the grain. Spoon over the Asian chimichurri and serve.

BOSS MOVE

Right before the final sear, hit that tri-tip with a light brush of toasted sesame oil. It boosts the crust, deepens the flavor, and ties that chimichurri back into the beef for a full-circle flavor bomb.

Smoked Braised Italian Oxtails

These are like the oxtails your granny used to make... if she smoked her oxtails and overdosed 'em with umami. We're talking big smoke, intoxicating aromas, and rich, fall-apart flavor that clings to polenta like it owes it money. It's rustic, refined, and delicious.

SERVES: 4 TO 6
PREP TIME: 30 MINUTES
SMOKE TIME: 2 HOURS
BRAISE TIME: 3 HOURS
TOTAL TIME: ABOUT 5½ HOURS (MOSTLY HANDS-OFF)

OXTAILS

4 pounds oxtails, cut and trimmed

2 tablespoons olive oil

1 tablespoon kosher salt

2 teaspoons black pepper

2 teaspoons mild all-purpose BBQ rub (optional)

Wood for smoking: oak or cherry

BRAISE

1 tablespoon olive oil

1 large yellow onion, diced

2 carrots, diced

2 celery stalks, diced

6 garlic cloves, smashed

2 tablespoons tomato paste

1 cup dry red wine

1 (28 oz) can San Marzano tomatoes, crushed

1 cup beef stock

1 tablespoon anchovy paste

1 teaspoon red pepper flakes

1 tablespoon balsamic vinegar (optional but adds a nice tang)

1 sprig rosemary

2 sprigs thyme

2 bay leaves

1 Parmesan rind (optional)

Zest of 1 lemon

Fresh parsley and grated Parmigiano-Reggiano, for garnish

SEASON THE OXTAILS: Rub the oxtails with olive oil, salt, pepper, and BBQ rub, if using. Let sit at room temperature while your smoker preheats.

SMOKE THE OXTAILS: Preheat the smoker to 250°F. Use oak or cherry wood. Smoke the oxtails for 2½ hours, flipping once halfway through. You want deep color, not fully cooked.

START THE BRAISE: In a large Dutch oven, heat the olive oil over medium heat. Add the onion, carrots, and celery. Cook for 8 to 10 minutes until soft. Stir in the garlic and tomato paste; cook for 2 to 3 minutes until the mixture darkens. Preheat the oven to 300°F.

BUILD THE SAUCE: Add the red wine, scrape the pot, and reduce the liquid by half, about 5 minutes. Add the crushed tomatoes, beef stock, anchovy paste, red pepper flakes, balsamic vinegar, herbs, and Parmesan rind, if using.

BRAISE THE OXTAILS: Nestle the smoked oxtails into the sauce. The liquid should come three-fourths of the way up the sides; add water if needed. Cover and braise in the oven for 3 hours, flipping the oxtails halfway, until fork-tender.

FINISH AND SERVE: Remove the oxtails from the sauce. Simmer the sauce uncovered on the stove to thicken, if desired. Discard the herbs and Parmesan rind. Stir in the lemon zest. Adjust the salt and pepper to taste.

GARNISH AND ENJOY: Top with fresh parsley and grated Parmigiano-Reggiano cheese.

BOSS MOVE

After the braise, toss in some roasted cherry tomatoes and a spoonful of Calabrian chili paste. The tomatoes hit with sweet and tangy vibes, and that chili paste brings smoky heat that turns the sauce into something magical. Serve over polenta, mashed potatoes, or pasta for an amazing dish!

Loaded Beefy Quesadilla

SERVES: 2 TO 3
COOK TIME: 25 MINUTES

Have you ever taken a bite of a quesadilla and gotten all cheese?! Then you take another bite and get all meat? Or all toppings?! This recipe right here solves that! A crispy, golden, perfectly toasted tortilla encompassing beefy, cheesy goodness in every bite. You won't ever make quesadillas another way.

FILLING

1 pound ground beef (or any cooked protein, such as steak, chicken, or pork)

One 1-ounce packet taco or Mexican seasoning or 2 to 3 tablespoons homemade

1 cup shredded cheddar cheese

1 cup shredded Monterey Jack or mozzarella cheese

1/3 cup diced onion (white or red)

1/2 cup chopped seeded tomato

1/4 cup chopped fresh cilantro

1/4 cup sour cream (optional)

1/4 cup salsa of choice, plus extra to serve

Guacamole and/or hot sauce, for serving (optional)

FOR ASSEMBLY

2 or 3 jumbo flour tortillas (burrito-size)

Neutral oil or unsalted butter, for the griddle

Flaky or kosher salt

COOK THE BEEF: In a skillet over medium heat, brown the ground beef. Once cooked, drain off the excess fat. Mix in the taco seasoning with 2 to 3 tablespoons of water. Let the mixture simmer for 1 to 2 minutes until it thickens and coats the meat. Remove from the heat and cool slightly.

MIX THE FILLING: In a large bowl, combine the seasoned beef, cheeses, onion, tomato, cilantro, sour cream, if using, and salsa. Mix thoroughly.

ASSEMBLE THE QUESADILLAS: Lay out a jumbo tortilla flat. Spoon a generous amount of the filling on half and fold the tortilla over it. Press gently.

GRIDDLE AND FLIP: Heat a large skillet or griddle over medium heat. Add a small amount of oil or butter. Place the quesadilla on the hot surface and lightly salt the top of the tortilla. Cook until golden brown, about 2 to 3 minutes, then carefully flip using a pizza paddle or large spatula. Toast the other side until crispy and the cheese is melty. Repeat for the remaining tortillas.

REST AND SLICE: Let the quesadillas rest for 1 to 2 minutes off the heat before slicing into wedges. Serve with salsa, guacamole, or hot sauce, if desired.

MAKE IT YOUR OWN: Use shredded rotisserie chicken or leftover carne asada. Toss in roasted corn, black beans, or pickled jalapeños. Get wild.

FLAVOR BOOST: Brush the outside of the tortilla with a quick garlic-butter blend before griddling. Mix just-melted butter, minced garlic, and a pinch of paprika or taco seasoning. It gives your quesadilla a golden crust that tastes like garlic bread and taco night had a baby.

Quick-Trip Ribeye with Italian Salsa Verde

People will often tell you not to flip your steak once you lay it on the grill. That if you want to build the perfect crust, you need to let it sit. WRONG! Constantly flip your steak. You're going to get an amazing crust and keep a nice pink interior. Punch it up with this Italian Salsa Verde, and you've got a steak fit for a backyard boss!!!

SERVES: 2
PREP TIME: 10 MINUTES
COOK TIME: 6 TO 8 MINUTES
REST TIME: 8 TO 10 MINUTES
TOTAL TIME: ABOUT 25 MINUTES

ITALIAN SALSA VERDE

½ cup chopped fresh Italian flat-leaf parsley

½ cup chopped fresh cilantro or chopped fresh parsley (if you don't like cilantro)

2 tablespoons capers, drained

2 anchovy fillets, minced

2 cloves garlic, minced

1 tablespoon Dijon mustard

2 tablespoons red wine vinegar

1 teaspoon freshly squeezed lemon juice

1 hard-boiled egg yolk, crumbled (for richness and body)

½ cup extra-virgin olive oil

½ teaspoon kosher salt, plus more as needed

¼ teaspoon freshly ground black pepper

½ teaspoon red pepper flakes (optional)

STEAK

One 16-ounce ribeye or New York strip steak (1 to 1¼ inches thick)

1½ teaspoons kosher salt

1 teaspoon freshly ground black pepper

MAKE THE SALSA VERDE: In a small bowl, mix the parsley, cilantro, if using, capers, anchovies, and garlic. In a medium bowl, whisk together the Dijon mustard, red wine vinegar, lemon juice, and crumbled egg yolk. Add the chopped herbs and aromatics. Slowly whisk in the olive oil until emulsified. Season with salt, pepper, and red pepper flakes, if using, to taste. Let it sit while you cook the steak.

GRILL THE STEAK: Preheat your grill for high direct heat. Season the steak generously with kosher salt and black pepper.

Grill using the quick-flip method—flip every 30 to 45 seconds over high heat. Rotate slightly on each flip for an even sear. Cook until the internal temperature hits 120°F for medium rare (6 to 8 minutes).

Remove from the grill and rest for 8 to 10 minutes. The steak's internal temperature will rise to about 130°F.

SLICE AND SERVE: Slice the steak against the grain, spoon *salsa verde* generously over the top, and serve immediately.

FLAVOR BOOST: For an extra layer of savory depth, gently warm the olive oil with a pinch of red pepper flakes and the minced garlic over low heat for a few minutes before whisking it into the other salsa ingredients. The infused oil adds a subtle warmth to the sauce.

A Word About Heat

Direct heat: Food is placed directly over the flames or coals to sear and cook quickly with high, radiant heat.

Indirect heat: Food is placed away from the heat source with the lid closed to roast slowly through circulating hot air.

Smoked Ropa Vieja

This is my wifes favorite dish, and I can see why. It's one of those dishes that invites you in as soon as you smell it, and then hugs you with every bite you take. I'm sure this doesn't compare to the version her abuela made for her growing up, but it makes her happy and she loves it. And for me, that's more than good enough.

SERVES: 6 TO 8 SERVINGS
PREP TIME: 15 MINUTES
COOK TIME: 2 HOURS (SMOKE) PLUS 2½ TO 3 HOURS (STOVETOP)

BEEF

2½ pounds chuck roast

3 cloves garlic, peeled

Kosher salt and freshly ground black pepper

½ teaspoon smoked paprika

Beef rub, such as SPG+ Rub (page 30), for smoking (optional)

SAUCE

3 cloves garlic, sliced

Two 8-ounce cans tomato sauce

One 28-ounce can crushed tomatoes

2 tablespoons tomato paste

1 green bell pepper, thinly sliced

1 medium onion, thinly sliced

One 4-ounce can chopped green chiles

2 teaspoons dried oregano

2 teaspoons kosher salt

1 tablespoon ground cumin

1 tablespoon white vinegar

½ cup dry white wine

½ teaspoons red pepper flakes

1 tablespoon Worcestershire sauce

1 teaspoon smoked paprika

Zest and juice of 1 lime

¼ cup chopped fresh cilantro, plus more for garnish

FOR FINISHING

½ cup coarsely chopped pimiento-stuffed green olives

PREP THE BEEF: Use a knife to cut three small X marks into the chuck roast. Press a whole garlic clove into each cut. Season all over with salt and pepper, then rub with smoked paprika and beef rub, if using.

SMOKE THE BEEF: Preheat the smoker until it reaches 250°F. Smoke the chuck roast at 250°F for 2 hours, or until it reaches an internal temperature of about 150°F.

BUILD THE BRAISE: Transfer the smoked beef to a large pot or Dutch oven on your stovetop. Add the garlic, tomato sauce, crushed tomatoes, tomato paste, bell pepper, onion, green chiles, oregano, salt, cumin, vinegar, white wine, red pepper flakes, Worcestershire sauce, smoked paprika, lime zest, and cilantro.

COOK ON STOVETOP: Bring the mixture to a gentle simmer over medium heat. Turn the heat to low, cover, and cook for 2½ to 3 hours, or until the beef is very fork-tender. Stir occasionally to prevent sticking.

SHRED AND FINISH: Shred the beef right in the pot using two forks. Stir it into the sauce, then add the olives. Taste for seasoning, adjusting if needed.

SERVE: Serve hot over white rice with Cuban-style black beans. Top with cilantro and a squeeze of fresh lime juice.

FLAVOR BOOST: Before shredding, pull the beef out and give it a quick sear in a hot skillet till it's crispy on the outside. Then toss it back in the sauce and shred it up. That little move adds crazy texture and next-level flavor.

Pineapple Express Steak with Charred Scallion Chimi

I used to say I'd never marinate a steak. Then I made this and that changed things forever. The grilled scallion and ginger chimi will have folks thinking you're Bobby Flay or somethin'. Easy peezy but damn delicious! This is the type of steak you'll want to eat right off the cutting board!

SERVES: 2
PREP TIME: 15 MINUTES
MARINATE TIME: 2 TO 4 HOURS
COOK TIME: 10 TO 12 MINUTES

STEAK AND MARINADE

½ cup pineapple juice

2 tablespoons soy sauce

1 tablespoon brown sugar

1 teaspoon sesame oil

1 clove garlic, minced

½ teaspoon grated fresh ginger

½ teaspoon freshly ground black pepper

1 ribeye or New York strip steak (1¼ to 1½ inches thick)

CHARRED SCALLION AND GINGER CHIMICHURRI

4 scallions

1-inch knob fresh ginger

¼ cup finely chopped fresh parsley

¼ cup finely chopped fresh cilantro

1 clove garlic, minced

¼ cup extra-virgin olive oil

1 tablespoon red wine vinegar

½ teaspoon red pepper flakes (optional)

Kosher salt

MARINATE THE STEAK: In a zip-top bag or baking dish, combine the pineapple juice, soy sauce, brown sugar, sesame oil, garlic, ginger, and black pepper. Add the ribeye and marinate in the fridge for 2 to 4 hours.

CHAR THE VEGETABLES: On a hot grill or in a hot skillet, char the scallions until blistered and blackened, 2 to 3 minutes. Peel and slice the ginger, then char the slices quickly, 1 to 2 minutes total. Let both cool slightly.

MAKE THE CHIMICHURRI: Finely chop the charred scallions and ginger and transfer to a medium bowl. Stir in the parsley, cilantro, garlic, olive oil, red wine vinegar, red pepper flakes, and salt to taste. Let it sit while the steak cooks.

GRILL THE STEAK: Setup a charcoal grill with a zone for direct and indirect heat. Remove the steak from the marinade (reserve the marinade, if you like, for the glaze) and pat dry. Grill over high heat, 4 to 5 minutes per side for medium rare. Flip frequently for a good crust. Rest for 10 minutes before slicing.

MAKE THE GLAZE (optional): Simmer the leftover marinade in a small pan over medium heat for 5 to 7 minutes, until thick and glossy. Brush it over the sliced steak.

SERVE: Slice the steak against the grain. Top with the charred scallion-ginger chimichurri. Serve with grilled pineapple, steamed rice, or tortillas if you're in taco mode.

BOSS MOVE

Toss in a spoonful of toasted cashews or peanuts! Trust me! The crunch and that nutty vibe plays perfectly with all the bright, smoky goodness going on in the chimi!

Cognac Cowboy Shanks

Beef shanks are like the less pretentious and more approachable cousin to oxtail. Packed with collagen and a deep-beef flavor... give 'em a little love and you've got something glorious. A little smoke, then let 'em soak in a rich cognac jacuzzi... this one smacks like it's wearing a pinkie ring. Pair with mashed potatoes, risotto, or creamy polenta.

SERVES: 4
PREP TIME: 30 MINUTES
SMOKE TIME: 1 HOUR
BRAISE TIME: 3 TO 3½ HOURS
TOTAL TIME: ABOUT 4½ HOURS

BEEF SHANKS

4 cross-cut beef shanks (1½ to 2 pounds total; 2 to 2½ inches thick with marrow bone)

2 tablespoons AP BBQ Rub (page 30)

1 tablespoon kosher salt

2 tablespoons neutral oil (such as avocado or canola, for searing if not smoking)

BRAISE

1 large yellow onion, chopped (about 1½ cups)

2 carrots, peeled and chopped (about 1 cup)

2 celery stalks, chopped (about 1 cup)

Pinch of kosher salt

8 cloves garlic, minced or crushed

2 tablespoons tomato paste

1 cup cognac (VS or VSOP)

3 cups beef stock (rich and low sodium), plus more as needed

½ tablespoon soy sauce

1 tablespoon Worcestershire sauce

4 or 5 sprigs fresh thyme

1 sprig fresh rosemary

1 bay leaf

1 teaspoon freshly ground black pepper

GARNISH (OPTIONAL)

Chopped fresh parsley or basil

Zest of 1 lemon

SMOKING YOUR SHANKS: Preheat your smoker to 275°F. Pat the shanks dry and season generously with the BBQ rub and salt. Smoke uncovered for 1 hour to develop a light bark. Pull and set aside.

NO SMOKER? SEAR INSTEAD: Heat the oil in a Dutch oven over medium-high heat. Sear the seasoned shanks for 4 to 5 minutes per side until deep golden brown. Remove and set aside.

BUILD THE BASE: In a Dutch oven (or large oven-safe pot), combine the chopped onion, carrots, and celery with a pinch of salt. Sauté until softened and caramelized, 8 to 10 minutes. Add the garlic and tomato paste and cook for 2 to 3 minutes more, letting the mixture darken in color and deepen in flavor. Preheat the oven to 300°F.

DEGLAZE AND BRAISE: Pour in the cognac and scrape up all the flavor bits from the bottom of the pot. Let reduce for 2 to 3 minutes. Stir in the beef stock, soy sauce, Worcestershire sauce, herbs, and pepper. Nestle the shanks back into the pot. The liquid should come about three-fourths of the way up the side. Top off with a splash of stock or water, if needed. Cover tightly and braise at 300°F in the oven (or continue in the smoker). Cook for 3 to 3½ hours, flipping once halfway through for even cooking. Shanks are done when they're fork-tender and pulling from the bone.

MAKE THE LOW AND SLOW MAGIC: Cover tightly and braise in the oven (or continue in the smoker) for 3 to 3½ hours, flipping once halfway through. Shanks are done when they're fork-tender and pulling away from the bone.

FINISH STRONG: Discard the herbs and skim off any excess fat. Remove the shanks. Bring the braising liquid to a boil and reduce for 5 to 10 minutes until it thickens slightly. Season to taste. Spoon the sauce over the shanks. Garnish with fresh parsley or basil and a hit of lemon zest for a citrusy pop.

SERVE LIKE A BOSS: Spoon the sauce over the shanks. Garnish with fresh parsley or basil and a hit of lemon zest for a citrusy pop. Pair with mashed potatoes, risotto, creamy polenta, or crusty bread.

FLAVOR BOOST: For an extra layer of umami and depth in your braising liquid, whisk in 1 tablespoon of Marmite or Vegemite after you've added the beef stock. It sounds crazy, but trust me.

Bullet Train Brisket

The first time I made this recipe, I had five hours to smoke a brisket: I was being judged by Rodney Scott, Brooke Williamson, and Carson Kressley, and it would air on national TV. Hopefully your situation is a little more relaxed. However, that doesn't mean you need to take eighteen hours to smoke a brisket. This recipe right here will have you in brisket paradise in no time!

SERVES: 12 TO 16
PREP TIME: 30 MINUTES
COOK TIME: 5 TO 6 HOURS
REST TIME: 1 TO 2 HOURS
TOTAL TIME: 6½ TO 8½ HOURS

EQUIPMENT

Drum smoker (I haven't perfected this on a pellet smoker or offset yet)

Instant-read meat thermometer

Butcher paper or heavy-duty foil (I lean toward foil when cooking at high heat)

Spray bottle

BRISKET

1 whole brisket, 12 to 15 pounds (prime grade preferably)

½ cup coarse salt

½ cup coarse black pepper

¼ cup garlic powder

½ cup beef broth

½ cup water

PREP THE BRISKET: Trim the brisket. Leave a ¼-inch fat cap on top. Square off thin edges and remove any hard fat or silver skin.

Apply the binder. Rub the mustard or fish sauce all over for adhesion and flavor depth. In a small bowl, combine the salt, pepper, garlic powder, and paprika or rub, if using, and thoroughly coat the meat with the spices.

Let it rest, either uncovered or loosely covered, in the fridge for at least 30 minutes or up to 3 hours while you fire up the smoker.

PREPARE THE BRISKET: Trim the brisket, removing the hard fat, any thin edges and the mohawk on top, leaving it uniform and even. Leave about ¼ inch of fat on the flat. Generously season all sides of the brisket with the rub (salt, pepper, and garlic powder). Let the brisket sit at room temperature for 30 minutes while you prepare the smoker.

PREHEAT THE SMOKER: Set up your drum smoker for indirect heat. Bring the temperature to a steady 325 to 350°F.

THE COOK (PART 1 - UNWRAPPED): Place the brisket directly on the grate, fat side down. Close the lid.

FLIP AND SPRITZ: After 30 to 45 minutes, open the smoker. Flip the brisket so the fat side is now up. In a spray bottle, combine the beef broth and water. Generously spritz the brisket. Continue to spritz and flip the brisket every 30 minutes for the next 2½ hours. Maintain the temperature of the smoker between 325°F to 350°F.

THE WRAP: Once the brisket has a dark, bark-like color and the internal temperature reaches approximately 165°F (Hopefully about 3½ hours into the cook), remove it from the smoker. Tightly wrap the brisket in a double layer of butcher paper or heavy-duty foil.

THE COOK (PART 2, WRAPPED): Return the wrapped brisket to the smoker (or put in your oven). Continue to cook until the internal temperature of the thickest part of the flat reaches 205°F to 212°F. This should take another 1½ hours. You are looking for a "probe-tender" feel, like sticking a skewer into a peanut butter.

THE REST: Remove the wrapped brisket from the smoker. Place it in a cooler, wrapped in a towel. A minimum rest of two hours is essential for the juices to redistribute, but if possible, letting it rest for 6 to 8 hours will make the brisket even more tender and juicy.

SLICE AND SERVE: After the rest, unwrap the brisket. Slice the flat against the grain and the point against its own grain. Serve immediately.

BOSS MOVE

After the brisket rests, slice it right before serving and brush those slices with that liquid gold, rendered fat from the wrap, or some warm tallow if you've got it. Don't waste the drippings, man. Coat that brizzy in all that juicy goodness.

Smoked Meatballs 'n' Marinara

Being adopted into an Italian American family means that, to me, spaghetti and meatballs for dinner were like a religious experience. Add in growing up in Napa/wine country, and I was surrounded by top-quality meatballs. This right here is my attempt at the best smoked meatballs you'll ever have.

SERVES: 6 TO 8
PREP TIME: 15 MINUTES
SMOKE TIME: 1 HOUR
SIMMER TIME: 20 MINUTES
TOTAL TIME: ABOUT 1 HOUR 35 MINUTES (PLUS SMOKER PREHEAT)

MEATBALLS

- 1 cup Italian-seasoned panko breadcrumbs
- ½ cup whole milk
- 2 pounds ground beef (80/20)
- ½ cup grated Parmigiano-Reggiano cheese
- 2 large eggs
- 6 cloves garlic, finely minced
- 1 small yellow onion, finely grated or minced
- 2 tablespoons chopped fresh parsley
- 1 tablespoon Worcestershire sauce
- 1 teaspoon dried oregano
- ½ tablespoon kosher salt
- ½ teaspoon freshly ground black pepper
- 1 teaspoon red pepper flakes (optional, for a touch of heat)

FOR SMOKING

Cherry, apple, pecan, or oak

TOMATO SAUCE

- ¼ cup extra-virgin olive oil
- 12 cloves garlic, thinly sliced
- 2 anchovy fillets, chopped (you can skip, but you shouldn't)
- 2 tablespoons capers, smashed
- 1 teaspoon red pepper flakes (optional)
- Two 28-ounce cans crushed or diced tomatoes
- Two 28-ounce cans tomato sauce
- 2 cups beef broth
- ¼ cup fresh oregano or 2 tablespoons dried
- Kosher salt and freshly ground black pepper
- 2 teaspoons sugar (optional, adjust for acidity)
- Fresh basil, to finish
- Grated Parmigiano-Reggiano cheese, to serve

PREP THE MEATBALLS: In a large bowl, mix together the breadcrumbs and milk. Let sit for 5 minutes until a paste forms.

Add the rest of the meatball ingredients. Mix gently with your hands until just combined. Don't overwork.

Form the meat mixture into golf ball-size meatballs and place on a wire rack set over a foil-lined sheet pan.

SMOKE THE MEATBALLS: Preheat your smoker to 250°F to 275°F. Smoke the meatballs for about 1 hour, or until they reach an internal temperature of 145°F to 150°F. Remove the meatballs from the smoker. They'll finish cooking in the sauce.

MAKE THE SAUCE: While the meatballs smoke, in a large Dutch oven or deep skillet, heat the olive oil over medium heat. Sauté the garlic and anchovies, if using, in the hot oil for 2 to 3 minutes until fragrant and golden. Add the capers and red pepper flakes, if using; stir briefly.

Pour in the crushed tomatoes, tomato sauce, and beef broth. Add the oregano, season with the salt and pepper to taste, and add the sugar, if needed. Simmer, uncovered, for 10 to 12 minutes, stirring occasionally, until the sauce is slightly thickened but still bright and fresh.

SIMMER THE MEATBALLS: Carefully nestle the smoked meatballs into the sauce. Spoon the sauce over them to coat. Cover and simmer on low for 20 minutes, until the meatballs are fully cooked through (165°F internal temperature, at least) and juicy.

FINISH AND SERVE: Top the meatballs and sauce with freshly torn basil and a generous handful of Parmigiano-Reggiano. Serve straight up, over pasta, or with toasted sourdough for dipping.

BOSS MOVE

Sauté your onion and garlic in a little olive oil till soft, let 'em cool, then mix 'em into your beef. It cuts the harsh bite, brings the sweetness, and makes those meatballs really sing.

The Chuck Roast

BBQ isn't fancy or pretentious. It's about time, love, and attention. This recipe right here is proof of that. After slow smoking and then braising, this tough cut that's full of connective tissue will melt in your mouth like butter. Fall-apart tender and packed with flavor... this is BBQ at its most deliciously basic level.

SERVES: 6 TO 8
PREP TIME: 15 MINUTES
SMOKE TIME: ABOUT 5 HOURS
BRAISE TIME: 2½ TO 3 HOURS
REST TIME: 30 MINUTES
TOTAL COOK TIME (EXCLUDING REST): 7½ TO 8 HOURS

CHUCK ROAST

One 3-to-4-pound boneless chuck roast

1 tablespoon yellow mustard

¼ cup coarse beef rub (your favorite or SPG+ Rub (page 30) or SPG Santa Maria Rub (page 79)

FOR SMOKING

Hickory, oak, pecan, or mesquite

BRAISE

1 yellow onion, thinly sliced

6 cloves garlic, smashed

1 sprig fresh rosemary

2 cups beef broth (preferably low sodium)

1 cup light beer or red wine, beef stock, or bourbon

2 tablespoons Worcestershire sauce (optional, but recommended)

PREP THE ROAST: Pat the roast dry. Slather it with mustard, which acts as a binder, then season all sides generously with the beef rub. Let the roast sit at room temperature while your smoker preheats.

SMOKE IT: Preheat your smoker to 250°F. Place the roast directly on the grates and smoke for about 5 hours, or until it hits an internal temperature of 160°F to 170°F and develops a rich, dark bark.

BUILD THE BRAISE: In a foil pan or Dutch oven, layer the sliced onion, smashed garlic, and rosemary sprig. Pour in the beef broth, beer (or other liquid), and Worcestershire sauce. Stir gently. Nestle the smoked chuck roast in the middle of the pan or pot.

BRAISE IT: Cover the pan or pot tightly with foil or a lid. Raise the smoker temperature to 275°F (or transfer to a 275°F oven) and braise for 2½ to 3 hours, or until the meat is fork-tender and reads about 205°F internal temperature.

REST AND SHRED: Let the roast rest in the braising liquid, still covered, for at least 30 minutes. Then shred, chunk, or slice and it's ready to serve. Spoon some of that smoky jus over the top for the ultimate finisher.

SERVE: Pile the sliced roast high over mashed potatoes or creamy polenta; make sandwiches with pickled onions and horseradish cream; or load it into tacos, quesadillas, or smoky beef nachos.

BOSS MOVE

After your chuck is smoked and braised, shred it up and toss it back into the reduced sauce with a knob of cold butter and a splash of vinegar or lemon juice. The combo of fat and acid makes it irresistible.

Mom's Red Stew

This one's the heart of the train. It's not just beef stew, it's straight-up comfort in a pot. Growing up, the smell of this used to fill the kitchen, and every bite still feels like a hug from Mom. It's rich, warm, and hits you right in the soul. Simple, nostalgic, and full of love, just how it's supposed to be.

SERVES: 6 TO 8
PREP TIME: 30 MINUTES
HANDS-ON TIME: 45 MINUTES
COOK TIME: 3 TO 3¼ HOURS
TOTAL TIME: 4 TO 4¼ HOURS

STEW

2½ pounds beef chuck, cut into 1½-inch cubes

1 tablespoon kosher salt

1 teaspoon freshly ground black pepper

3 tablespoons extra-virgin olive oil, divided

1 large yellow onion, finely chopped

2 celery stalks, diced

8 cloves garlic, minced

2 tablespoons tomato paste

1 cup dry red wine (Chianti or Sangiovese recommended)

One 28-ounce can whole San Marzano tomatoes, crushed by hand

2 cups beef stock

2 tablespoons Italian seasoning

1 bay leaf

1 small bunch fresh thyme, 5 or 6 sprigs

Pinch of red pepper flakes (optional, but encouraged)

VEGETABLES

1 pound baby carrots

1 to 1½ pounds baby potatoes, halved, if large

1 heaping cup frozen green beans or peas

FOR FINISHING

Kosher salt and freshly ground black pepper

Chopped fresh parsley or basil

Freshly grated Parmesan cheese

BROWN THE BEEF: Pat the beef dry and season it with salt and pepper. Heat 2 tablespoons of the olive oil in a heavy pot or Dutch oven over medium-high heat. Sear the beef in batches in the hot oil until browned on all sides. Remove the beef and set aside.

BUILD THE BASE: Add the remaining 1 tablespoon olive oil to the pot. Toss in the onion and celery and cook until soft and golden, 5 to 7 minutes. Add the garlic and tomato paste; stir for 2 minutes until fragrant and caramelized.

DEGLAZE AND SIMMER: Pour in the red wine, scraping the bottom of the pot to lift all those flavorful browned bits. Let it reduce by half, about 5 minutes. Add the hand-crushed tomatoes, beef stock, Italian seasoning, bay leaf, thyme sprigs, and red pepper flakes, if using. Stir to combine.

SLOW COOK THE MAGIC: Return the seared beef to the pot and add the baby carrots. Bring to a simmer, then cover and cook over low heat for 1½ to 2 hours, stirring occasionally.

ADD POTATOES: Stir in the baby potatoes. Cover and simmer for another 40 minutes, or until both the beef and potatoes are fork-tender.

FINISH WITH GREENS: In the last 10 to 15 minutes of cooking, stir in the frozen green beans (or peas). Let them heat through without overcooking.

TASTE AND SERVE: Remove the bay leaf and thyme stems. Taste and adjust the salt and pepper as needed. Serve hot in bowls, garnished with fresh parsley or basil and a healthy sprinkle of Parmesan cheese.

FLAVOR BOOST: For an even deeper, richer umami kick, before adding your beef stock and tomatoes, stir in 1 tablespoon miso paste, either white or yellow, with your tomato paste and garlic. Whisk it in with ½ red wine until dissolved. It will add an incredible layer of savory complexity to the broth without tasting distinctly like miso.

BOSS MOVE

Stir a spoon of miso into your tomato paste, garlic, and red wine before the stock hits. It blends smooth and loads the broth with a deep, savory flavor that's stupid delicious.

Hot Umami SmashBurger

I love smashburgers. I mean, who doesn't?! I also love sriracha, so I figured why not combine two things I enjoy and see what happens? The result was this bodacious burger. Spicy, sweet, savory, and tangy. This burger right here checks all the boxes. Keep a glass of cold water nearby . . . this one brings the heat!

SERVES: 2
PREP TIME: 5 MINUTES
COOK TIME: 10 TO 15 MINUTES
TOTAL TIME: 15 TO 20 MINUTES

SPICY MISO CARAMELIZED ONIONS

2 tablespoons unsalted butter

1 tablespoon neutral oil (grapeseed, avocado, canola or vegetable)

2 large yellow onions, thinly sliced

Pinch of kosher salt

2 tablespoons white miso paste

2 tablespoons sriracha (I like Melinda's)

2 tablespoons brown sugar

1 tablespoon rice vinegar

SMASH PATTIES

1 pound ground beef (80/20 recommended)

Neutral oil or beef fat, for the griddle

Kosher salt and freshly ground black pepper

4 slices American or pepper Jack cheese

SRIRACHA MAYO

¼ cup mayonnaise

1 tablespoon sriracha, or more as needed

½ teaspoon freshly squeezed lime juice

FOR ASSEMBLY

2 soft burger buns

Pickles (recommended)

Shredded iceberg lettuce or arugula (optional)

MAKE THE MISO ONIONS: Heat the butter and oil in a skillet over medium heat. Add the onions and a pinch of salt. Cook for 8 to 10 minutes, stirring frequently, until the onions are soft and golden brown. Stir in the miso paste, sriracha, brown sugar, and rice vinegar. Cook for 2 to 3 minutes more until the mixture is thick and glossy. Set aside and keep warm.

SMASH THE BURGERS: Divide the ground beef into 4 equal portions of ¼ pound each. Gently form into loose balls; do not overwork the meat.

Heat a cast-iron skillet or griddle over high heat until smoking hot. Add a small amount of oil or beef fat.

Place 2 beef balls on the hot surface, spaced apart. Place a piece of parchment paper on top of each beef ball, to prevent sticking when smashed. Using a sturdy spatula or burger press, smash each ball flat into a thin patty.

Season generously with salt and pepper.

Cook for 1½ to 2 minutes, until deeply browned and crispy at the edges. Flip the patties, season the other side, and immediately top each with a slice of cheese. Cook for 1 minute or so, until the cheese is melted. Repeat with the 2 remaining beef balls.

ASSEMBLE: Toast the burger buns. In a small bowl, mix the sriracha mayo ingredients. Spread generously on both sides of the toasted buns. Stack two cheesy patties per burger on the bottom bun. Top with a generous pile of the spicy miso caramelized onions. Add pickles and greens, if using. Cap it off with the top bun and serve immediately.

FLAVOR BOOST: Right after smashing those patties, hit the hot griddle with a splash of rice vinegar or pickle juice around the edges. It'll steam up and blend into the beef, adding a tangy punch that plays well with the richness.

LEVEL UP: Stack that double while the second patty's still sizzling so the cheese melts everything together into one glorious mess.

Black Magic Beef Ribs

Beef ribs are one of the best bites in BBQ... basically brisket on a stick. And truthfully, they don't need much. However, if you want something out of this world, hit 'em with this black magic glaze. It'll unlock a level of flavor that you didn't think was possible.

SERVES: 4 TO 6
PREP TIME: 15 MINUTES
COOK TIME: 6 TO 7 HOURS (5 TO 6 HOURS SMOKING PLUS GLAZE TIME)
REST TIME: 20 TO 30 MINUTES

RIBS

One 4-to-5 pound rack full-plate beef ribs

¼ cup Worcestershire sauce

¼ cup yellow mustard (optional)

3 to 4 tablespoons of your favorite beef rub (coarse and peppery recommended)

2 cups beef broth or water (for spritzing: optional)

FOR SMOKING

Something bold, such as oak or hickory

BLACK MAGIC GLAZE

½ cup Worcestershire sauce (Bear & Burton's is my go-to)

¼ cup packed light brown sugar

2 tablespoons soy sauce

2 tablespoons balsamic vinegar

1 tablespoon spicy brown or hot mustard

2 cloves garlic, minced

1 tablespoon unsalted butter

PREP THE RIBS: Pat the ribs dry. If there's a thick membrane on the bone side, remove it for better tenderness. Coat the rib with Worcestershire sauce and mustard, if using, to help the rub stick. Season generously with your beef rub, covering all sides. Let sit for 30 minutes at room temperature or up to 2 to 3 hours in the fridge.

SMOKE LOW AND SLOW: Preheat your smoker to 275°F. Place the ribs bone-side down on the smoker grates. Let them smoke for 5 to 6 hours, or until probe-tender (internal temperature should be 200°F to 205°F). If you like, spritz with beef broth or water every hour after the first 2 hours if they look dry to help keep them juicy.

MAKE THE GLAZE: About 45 minutes before the ribs are done, combine all the glaze ingredients in a saucepan over medium heat. Simmer for 10 to 15 minutes, stirring occasionally, until the glaze is thick and glossy. Be careful not to scorch it.

GLAZE 'EM UP: During the last 30 minutes of your cook, brush the ribs generously with the Black Magic Glaze. Let the glaze tack up and caramelize on the surface. You can apply a second coat after 15 minutes if desired.

REST AND SLICE: Once tender and glossy, pull the ribs from the smoker. Tent them loosely with foil and let them rest for 20 to 30 minutes. Slice between the bones and serve them up hot. Drizzle and dip for extra enjoyment.

FLAVOR BOOST: Right before you glaze, hit those ribs with a quick butter baste. Melt some butter with garlic and herbs, brush it on, then glaze. That buttery layer locks in shine and makes the glaze pop like crazy.

Full Send Flanken Ribs

Marinated flanken ribs are one of my all-time favorites. They're easy to prep, loaded with Asian influence, and built to soak up every ounce of flavor you throw at 'em. Thin-cut, tender, and packed with that juicy bite, they're just hella fun to eat, whether you're grabbing them hot off the grill or tearing into a pile with friends.

SERVES: 4
PREP TIME: 10 MINUTES
MARINATE TIME: AT LEAST 3 HOURS, PREFERABLY OVERNIGHT
GRILL TIME: 4 TO 6 MINUTES

MARINADE
1 cup soy sauce
½ cup Shaoxing wine
½ cup sriracha (Melinda's is my fav)
½ cup sweet and spicy Polynesian sauce (I like Melinda's), or ½ cup sweet chili sauce
1 tablespoon sesame oil
8 cloves garlic, minced
½ white onion, grated
2 tablespoons ground ginger

RIBS
3 pounds flanken-style beef short ribs (about ½ inch thick)

GARNISH (OPTIONAL)
Finely chopped scallions
Sesame seeds

MAKE THE MARINADE: In a large bowl or zip-top bag, combine all the marinade ingredients. Mix well until evenly blended.

MARINATE THE RIBS: Add the flanken short ribs to the marinade and coat thoroughly. Seal and refrigerate for at least 3 hours, preferably overnight, for maximum flavor.

PREHEAT THE GRILL: Get your grill very hot—high direct heat, around 450°F to 500°F.

GRILL THE RIBS: Remove the ribs from the marinade and let any excess drip off. Grill the ribs for 2 to 3 minutes per side, flipping once, until nicely charred and caramelized. Because they're thin-cut, they cook fast—don't walk away!

REST AND SERVE: Let the ribs rest for a few minutes, then slice between the bones, if needed. Garnish with scallions or sesame seeds, if desired.

BOSS MOVE
Right off the grill, hit those ribs with a quick honey-soy brush (2-to-1 ratio). The heat melts it into a sticky, glossy glaze that slaps you with sweet-savory goodness and takes 'em straight to flavor town station.

Smoked Ossobuco

Smoked then slow-braised veal shanks that fall right off the bone! This is where BBQ swagger meets Old World elegance. They soak up that buttery, wine-kissed sauce like a sponge, bringing deep smoke and melt-in-your-mouth tenderness together in perfect harmony. Hit it with a zesty gremolata to wake it all up, and you've got fine dining flavor that still feels like straight-up comfort food.

SERVES: 4
PREP TIME: 30 MINUTES
COOK TIME: 6 HOURS
TOTAL TIME: 2½ HOURS

FOR THE BEEF SHANKS

4 beef ossobuco cuts (cross-cut beef shanks, about 1½ to 2 inches thick)

1 tablespoon olive oil

2 teaspoons kosher salt, plus more as needed

1 teaspoon black pepper, plus more as needed

1 small carrot, diced (½ cup)

1 celery stalk, diced (½ cup)

½ medium yellow onion, chopped (½ cup)

3 tablespoons unsalted butter, divided

⅔ cup dry red wine (beef pairs better with red wine than white)

1¼ cups beef stock (or a mix of beef and bone broth), plus more as needed

Kitchen twine

1 teaspoon lemon zest (1 lemon)

2 tablespoons finely chopped, fresh flat-leaf parsley

½ small clove garlic, finely minced or grated

SMOKE: Pat the beef shanks dry. Tie each piece with kitchen twine. Rub with the olive oil, 1 teaspoon of the salt, and ½ teaspoon of the pepper. Preheat your smoker to 225°F to 250°F. Smoke the beef shanks for 2 to 2½ hours until the bark forms.

SAUTÉ AND BRAISE: In a large Dutch oven, melt 1 tablespoon of butter over medium heat. Add the carrot, celery, and onion. Sauté for 8 to 10 minutes until soft. Season with the remaining 1 teaspoon salt and ½ teaspoon pepper. Add your smoked beef shanks to the pot. Pour in the red wine, bring to a simmer, and cook for 5 to 7 minutes, scraping up any browned bits (fond). Add the beef stock (the liquid should almost cover the meat). Bring to a gentle simmer. Cover the pot and transfer to a preheated 325°F oven. Braise for 3½ to 4½ hours, or until the meat is extremely tender and easily falling off the bone. Gently turn the meat halfway through.

FINISH AND SERVE: Carefully remove the beef shanks (remove the twine) and keep them warm. If the sauce is too thin, simmer it uncovered on the stovetop until slightly reduced. Turn off the heat. Whisk in the remaining 1½ tablespoons of butter until smooth. Taste and adjust seasoning. Mix the lemon zest, parsley, and garlic. Stir about half of this mixture into the finished sauce. Place a beef shank on a plate. Spoon the rich, smoky sauce over the meat and sprinkle with the remaining fresh gremolata.

BOSS MOVE

Serve it with creamy cheesy risotto, but stir a spoonful of that ossobuco sauce right into the rice first. It loads every bite with that deep, meaty flavor.

DIXXON

CHAPTER 2

POULTRY

CLUCKIN' FREIGHT

Okay, folks, on this part of the ride, chicken doesn't play second fiddle. It's the star of the show. This chapter is stacked with smoky wings, juicy thighs, crispy tenders, and saucy sandwiches that prove poultry isn't just a blank canvas. It's a Flavor Train waiting to fly off the rails. You'll get recipes that range from boozy glazes to bold global spins, all designed to turn your grill into a five-star chicken shack. Whether you're working with a whole bird, boneless cuts, or wings by the dozen, this is where your inner pitmaster learns to treat chicken right with fire, finesse, and a whole lotta flavor.

Flavor Packin,
Never Lackin'

Peach Lollipop Chicken

These chicken lollipops are candy on a bone, dipped in a sweet, sticky peach glaze that delivers the goods every bite! Tasty enough to win a competition or get sold at the local candy shop. These are guaranteed to have both kids and grown folks going at 'em till the plate's licked clean.

SERVES: 4 TO 6 (MAKES 10 DRUMSTICKS)

PREP TIME: 20 TO 30 MINUTES (FOR LOLLIPOPPING)

COOK TIME: ABOUT 1 HOUR 30 MINUTES

CHICKEN

10 chicken drumsticks

2 tablespoons yellow mustard (optional)

1½ tablespoons brisket-style rub or AP BBQ Rub (page 30)

1 tablespoon peach-forward BBQ rub (I like Heath Riles, or any sweet rub)

FOR SMOKING

Peach, apple, or cherry

PEACH KETCHUP GLAZE

¾ cup peach preserves

½ cup ketchup

2 tablespoons apple cider vinegar

1 tablespoon brown sugar

1 tablespoon Worcestershire sauce

1 tablespoon Dijon or yellow mustard

½ teaspoon garlic powder

Squeeze of fresh lemon juice (to brighten and balance)

PREP THE LOLLIPOPS: Using a sharp knife, cut through the skin and tendons around the narrow end (ankle) of each drumstick, 1 to 1½ inches from the tip of the bone. Push the meat down toward the thick end of the drumstick to form a "lollipop" shape. Remove the knuckle tip (cartilage and small bones at the very end) for a flatter base, if desired, and trim any exposed tendons or loose skin for a clean look. (Optional: Remove the skin from the exposed bone part for a cleaner bite and better glaze grip.)

TO SEASON: Rub the drumsticks with yellow mustard as a binder, if using. In a small bowl, mix the brisket rub and peach rub. Season the drumsticks generously with this fifty-fifty blend. Let sit at room temperature while you heat up the smoker.

TO SMOKE: Preheat your smoker to 275°F. Stand the drumsticks upright in a drumstick rack or create a foil ring to help them stand in the smoker. Smoke for 1 to 1 hour 15 minutes, or until the skin is tight and starting to crisp.

Note: You'll likely go past 165°F internal temperature to tighten and crisp the skin—that's okay. Drumsticks are dark meat and stay juicy even at 180°F to 190°F.

FOR THE PEACH GLAZE: While drumsticks smoke, combine all the glaze ingredients in a small saucepan. Simmer over low heat for 5 to 8 minutes, stirring often, until thick and glossy. Pour the hot glaze into a tall glass or wide-mouth jar suitable for dunking.

TO DUNK AND FINISH: Remove the drumsticks from the smoker. Carefully dunk each one into the glaze, twisting to coat completely. Return the glazed drumsticks to the smoker for another 10 minutes to let the glaze tack up and set.

TO SERVE: Let rest for 5 minutes, then stack 'em up and serve. Dunk again in any remaining warm glaze before serving for double gloss and extra flavor, if you'd like.

BOSS MOVE

After smoking the drumsticks, crank your grill or oven to 400°F and hit 'em on a wire rack for 10 to 15 minutes before glazing. That two-step crisp locks in extra bite and bark that'll have you hooked.

Cognac Wings a.k.a. Grown-Folk Wings

These cognac-glazed wings bring together everything I love about BBQ: smoky, sticky, boozy, and crazy easy to make. I'm partial to Tycoon cognac, but you do you. Perfect wings, perfect glaze, and they smack even harder with some Bay Area slaps bumpin' in the background.

SERVES: 4

PREP TIME: 15 MINUTES PLUS AT LEAST 30 MINUTES MARINATING

COOK TIME: 45 TO 90 MINUTES, DEPENDING ON METHOD

WINGS

2 pounds chicken wings, drums and flats separated

1 tablespoon extra-virgin olive oil

2 tablespoons SPG+ Rub (page 30), or your favorite chicken rub

COGNAC GLAZE

½ cup ketchup

¼ cup cognac (Tycoon Spirits, or whatever brand you like)

3 tablespoons honey

2 tablespoons apple cider vinegar

1 tablespoon Worcestershire sauce

1 tablespoon yellow mustard

1 teaspoon soy sauce

½ teaspoon onion powder

½ teaspoon garlic powder

¼ teaspoon red pepper flakes or a few dashes of your favorite hot sauce (optional, for heat)

SEASON THE WINGS: Pat the wings dry with paper towels. In a large bowl, toss the chicken wings with the olive oil and SPG+ Rub until evenly coated. Marinate at room temperature for at least 30 minutes. For maximum flavor, cover and refrigerate overnight.

Cook the wings (choose your method):

GRILL: Preheat your grill, setting up for two-zone heat (direct and indirect) at approximately 375°F. Place the wings on the indirect heat side and cook for 30 to 40 minutes, flipping halfway through, until they're looking crispy, have pull back from the bone and are between 175° to 185°F internal. Move the wings to the direct heat side for the last 2 to 3 minutes per side to achieve a crispy char.

OVEN: Preheat your oven to 400°F. Arrange the wings in a single layer on a wire rack set over a baking sheet (this allows air to circulate for crispier skin). Bake for 45 to 50 minutes, flipping the wings once about halfway through. For extra crispiness, you can broil them for 2 to 3 minutes at the end, watching very carefully to prevent burning.

SMOKER: Preheat your smoker to 300°F. Place the wings directly on the smoker grates. Smoke for 1 hour, or until the wings are cooked through and the skin is crisped to your liking.

MAKE THE COGNAC GLAZE: In a small saucepan, combine the ketchup, cognac, honey, apple cider vinegar, Worcestershire sauce, yellow mustard, soy sauce, onion powder, garlic powder, and red pepper flakes or hot sauce to taste. Simmer 8 to 10 minutes over medium heat until glossy and slightly thickened. Adjust seasoning if needed, then cool slightly.

GLAZE AND FINISH: Once the wings are cooked through and crispy, transfer them to a large bowl. Pour the warm cognac glaze over the top and toss gently until they are generously and evenly coated. Plate immediately and enjoy, or you can return the wings to the smoker/grill/oven after tossing in sauce to cook a few minutes more to caramelize.

FLAVOR BOOST: Splash a little cognac into the sauce off the heat for that smooth, boozy kick. Then hit your glazed wings with crispy fried shallots and sesame seeds. It's gonna make these wings "extra" in the best way!

When Are They Ready?

Wings hit perfection at 175° to 185°F internal. Higher temp makes them tender and pull-off-the-bone clean. Visually, look for golden, tight, crispy skin. No pale, rubbery vibes. Give a drum a little wiggle. If the bone moves easy and the juices run clear, you're good.

Maple Bacon Chicken Wings

I flipped wings into a breakfast vibe with maple syrup, crispy bacon, and that sweet smoky magic . . . yet somehow they still hit like dessert. No joke, these are unforgettable. Breakfast, dessert, and wings all on one plate. Trust, your crew will be talking about 'em long after these are gone.

SERVES: 4

PREP TIME: AT LEAST 30 MINUTES (OR OVERNIGHT)

COOK TIME (WINGS): ABOUT 45 TO 60 MINUTES

GLAZE TIME: 10 MINUTES

FINISH TIME: 5 MINUTES

TOTAL TIME (EXCLUDING REST): 1 HOUR TO 1 HOUR 15 MINUTES

WINGS

2½ to 3 pounds chicken wings (about 10 to 15 pieces)

1 tablespoon aluminum-free baking powder

MAPLE BACON GLAZE

½ cup pure maple syrup

¼ cup packed light brown sugar

2 tablespoons soy sauce

1 tablespoon Dijon mustard

1 teaspoon apple cider vinegar

½ teaspoon red pepper flakes (optional, for heat)

4 slices thick-cut bacon

Sliced scallions, for garnish

PREP AND DRY-BRINE THE WINGS: Pat the wings very dry with paper towels. Drier wings result in crispier skin. In a large bowl, toss the wings with the baking powder, kosher salt, garlic powder, smoked paprika, and black pepper until evenly coated.

Arrange the wings in a single layer on a wire rack set over a sheet pan. Let them rest in the fridge, uncovered, for at least 30 minutes (or ideally overnight) to help dry out the skin.

Cook the wings (choose your method):

SMOKER/GRILL (PREFERRED): Preheat your smoker or grill to 275°F. Smoke/grill the wings (indirect heat) for 45 to 60 minutes, flipping halfway, until the internal temperature hits 175°F plus and the skin is rendered and slightly crisp.

OVEN: Preheat your oven to 425°F. Bake the wings on a wire rack over a foil-lined baking sheet for 45 to 50 minutes, flipping halfway through.

AIR FRYER: Set the air fryer to 380°F for 24 minutes and add the wings, flipping at 12 minutes. Then increase the temperature to 400°F for 5 minutes more to finish crisping.

MAKE THE MAPLE BACON GLAZE: While the wings cook, in a small saucepan, combine the maple syrup, brown sugar, soy sauce, mustard, vinegar, and red pepper flakes (if using).

Simmer over medium heat for 5 to 7 minutes, stirring occasionally, until slightly thickened. Meanwhile, cook the bacon in a separate skillet over medium heat until crispy. Drain on paper towels, then finely chop. Reserve 1 tablespoon of the rendered bacon fat.

Stir the chopped cooked bacon and reserved bacon fat into the maple glaze. Remove from the heat.

GLAZE AND FINISH: Once the wings are cooked and crispy, transfer them to a large bowl. Pour the warm maple bacon glaze over the hot wings and toss until fully coated. Return the glazed wings to the smoker, oven (still at 425°F), or grill (direct heat for 1 to 2 minutes) for about 5 minutes to allow the glaze to set and caramelize slightly.

SERVE: Plate the wings and sprinkle with extra crispy bacon bits (if you have any left!) or sliced scallions if desired. Serve hot and sticky.

BOSS MOVE

For extra crunch and savor, during the final glazing stage, sprinkle 1 tablespoon of crushed pork rinds directly onto the wings. Crispity, crunchety, and intensely savory.

Tequila Lime Wings

Tequila Lime Wings are basically a party on a plate. They've got that tequila kick, a citrusy punch of lime, and wings that are way too easy to smash on. Warning: They may cause spontaneous dancing or you yelling, "One more round!" before the wings are even gone.

SERVES: 3 TO 4
PREP TIME: 15 MINUTES
MARINATE TIME: 4 TO 24 HOURS
COOK TIME: 30 TO 40 MINUTES

WINGS AND MARINADE

1¼ cup silver tequila

6 cloves garlic, smashed

2 tablespoons soy sauce

1½ tablespoons Tajín plus extra for garnish

1 tablespoon kosher salt

1 tablespoon freshly ground black pepper

1½ tablespoons freshly squeezed lime juice (about ½ lime)

1½ teaspoons lime zest plus extra for garnish

2 pounds chicken party wings

POST-MARINADE SEASONING

1 ½ teaspoons seasoned salt

1 teaspoon chipotle powder

GLAZE

⅓ cup silver tequila (I like Santo and E. Cuarenta)

¼ cup freshly squeezed lime juice (3 to 4 limes)

½ cup honey

2 tablespoons brown sugar

2 tablespoons soy sauce

1 tablespoon of your favorite hot sauce

3 cloves garlic, minced

2 teaspoons lime zest

Pinch of salt

GARNISH

Small bunch cilantro, finely chopped (optional)

Lime zest (optional)

MARINATE THE WINGS: In a large bowl or zip-top bag, combine the silver tequila, smashed garlic, soy sauce, Tajín, salt, pepper, fresh lime juice, and lime zest. Add the wings and mix to coat. Marinate in the refrigerator for at least 4 hours, ideally overnight.

PREHEAT THE SMOKER OR GRILL: Preheat your smoker or grill to 350°F, set up for indirect heat.

DRY AND SEASON: Remove the wings from the marinade, discard the marinade, and pat the wings dry with paper towels to help the skin crisp up. Season with the seasoned salt and chipotle powder.

COOK THE WINGS: Place the wings on the smoker or grill (indirect heat) and cook for 30 to 40 minutes, flipping once halfway through if needed. Cook until the internal temperature reaches at least 165°F, but more importantly, until the skin is crisp.

MAKE THE GLAZE: While the wings are cooking, add the tequila, lime juice, honey, brown sugar, soy sauce, hot sauce, minced garlic, lime zest, and salt to a small saucepan over medium heat. Bring to a simmer, then lower the heat and cook for 5 to 10 minutes, stirring occasionally, until reduced and sticky.

GLAZE AND FINISH: Once the wings are done, toss them in the warm glaze or brush it on generously. Garnish with chopped fresh cilantro, lime zest, or even a sprinkle of Tajín if desired.

FLAVOR BOOST: Glaze the wings, hit 'em with lime zest and a hot honey drip, then let the fireworks go off!!! Serve with more lime wedges on the side so folks can let the juice loose every bite.

BOSS MOVE

Save a little glaze for dipping. It's also amazing on grilled shrimp or even corn.

Lemon Pepper Buffalo Chicken Tenders with Homemade Blue Cheese Ranch

SERVES: 4
PREP TIME: 15 MINUTES
MARINATE TIME: 30 MINUTES TO OVERNIGHT
FRY TIME: ABOUT 15 MINUTES
TOTAL TIME (EXCLUDING MARINATING)**:** ABOUT 30 MINUTES

I have no desire to build a fast-food empire, but if I did, this recipe would be what I built the business on. There's nothing bland about this chicken. Juicy, tender, tasty, crispy, and delicious. And if you can't decide if you like blue cheese or ranch, you're in luck: With this recipe, you don't have to choose.

CHICKEN AND MARINADE

1 cup buttermilk

1 tablespoon Bear & Burton's Fireshire or Worcestershire sauce

1½ pounds chicken tenders

HOMEMADE BLUE CHEESE RANCH

½ cup mayonnaise

½ cup sour cream

¼ cup buttermilk, plus more to thin, if needed

⅓ cup blue cheese, crumbled

1 clove garlic, minced

1 tablespoon freshly squeezed lemon juice or white vinegar

1 teaspoon dried dill

½ teaspoon onion powder

Kosher salt and freshly ground black pepper

DREDGE

1 cup all-purpose flour

½ cup cornstarch

1 tablespoon lemon pepper

1 teaspoon garlic powder

1 teaspoon paprika

½ teaspoon kosher salt

½ teaspoon freshly ground black pepper

FOR FRYING

Neutral oil (such as canola, vegetable, or peanut)

LEMON PEPPER BUFFALO SAUCE

¼ cup unsalted butter

¾ cup buffalo hot sauce (I like Frank's RedHot)

Juice of ½ lemon

1 tablespoon Lemon Pepper Herb Rub (page 31)

1 teaspoon lemon pepper

MARINATE THE CHICKEN: In a bowl, mix the buttermilk and Fireshire. Add the chicken tenders and turn to ensure they are coated. Cover and refrigerate for at least 30 minutes, or overnight for maximum flavor.

MAKE THE HOMEMADE BLUE CHEESE RANCH: In a bowl, combine the mayo, sour cream, buttermilk, crumbled blue cheese, minced garlic clove, lemon juice, dried dill, onion powder, and salt and pepper to taste. Mix until smooth.

Chill for at least 15 minutes for the best flavor. Thin with a little more buttermilk if needed to reach the desired consistency.

MIX THE DREDGE: In a shallow dish, combine the flour, cornstarch, lemon pepper, garlic powder, paprika, salt, and pepper.

BREAD THE TENDERS: Remove the chicken tenders from the buttermilk marinade, letting the excess drip off. Dip each tender into the dredge mixture, then back into the buttermilk, and finally back into the dredge, pressing the coating on well to ensure a thick, crispy crust.

FRY 'EM UP: Heat 1 to 2 inches of neutral oil to 350°F in a deep pan or fryer over medium-high heat. Fry the tenders in batches for 5 to 7 minutes per batch, until golden brown and cooked through (internal temperature of 165°F). Drain on a wire rack or paper towels.

MAKE THE LEMON PEPPER BUFFALO SAUCE: In a small saucepan over low heat, melt the butter. Stir in the buffalo hot sauce, lemon juice, citrus BBQ rub, and lemon pepper rub. Warm through, then remove from the heat.

TOSS AND SERVE: In a large bowl, toss the crispy tenders in the warm lemon pepper buffalo sauce until evenly coated. Serve immediately with the homemade blue cheese ranch.

FLAVOR BOOST: When the buffalo sauce comes off the heat, stir in some honey and a squeeze of lemon. It'll sharpen the flavor and add a subtle sweetness that definitely ups the crave factor!

Smoked Fried Buffalo Flappers

Buffalo wings are already all time... But smoke 'em first? Then fry 'em?! GAME OVER!!! The smoke brings added flavor, the fry locks in a bomb-ass crispy crunch, and the buffalo sauce brings the messy heat. Finger-lickin', last-wing-fightin'... These are guaranteed to be your game-day go-to!

SERVES: 3 TO 4
PREP TIME: 1 TO 2 HOURS, OR OVERNIGHT
SMOKE TIME: ABOUT 1½ HOURS
FRY TIME: 2 TO 3 MINUTES PER BATCH
TOTAL TIME (EXCLUDING AIR-DRY): ABOUT 2 HOURS

WINGS

2½ pounds chicken party wings (18 to 20 wings), separated into flats and drums

2 tablespoons SPG+ Rub (page 30), or your favorite chicken rub

½ teaspoon baking powder (it helps crisp them up)

FOR SMOKING

I like cherry, apple or pecan

BUFFALO SAUCE

6 tablespoons unsalted butter

1 tablespoon honey

½ cup Bear & Burton's Special Reserve Everyday Hot Sauce or your favorite cayenne hot sauce

½ tablespoon white vinegar

1 teaspoon Worcestershire sauce

1 teaspoon garlic powder

¼ teaspoon cayenne pepper (optional, for extra kick)

FOR FRYING

2 to 3 quarts neutral oil (such as canola or peanut)

FOR SERVING

Ranch or blue cheese dressing and celery sticks

SEASON AND AIR-DRY: Pat the wings thoroughly dry with paper towels. In a large bowl, toss the wings with your rub and baking powder until evenly coated. Lay them out on a wire rack set over a baking sheet and let them air-dry in the fridge, uncovered, for 1 to 2 hours (or overnight for maximum crispness).

SMOKE 'EM: Preheat your smoker to 250°F. Smoke the wings for about 1½ hours, or until they reach an internal temperature of 165°F. They should be cooked through and smoky, but not crispy.

FRY 'EM UP: Heat the oil to 375°F in a deep pot or deep fryer over medium-high heat. Carefully fry the smoked wings in batches for 2 to 3 minutes per batch, until golden brown and the skin is shatteringly crisp. Drain on a clean wire rack (not paper towels) to maintain their crunch.

MAKE THE BUFFALO SAUCE: In a saucepan over medium-low heat, melt the butter. Add the hot sauce, honey, vinegar, Worcestershire sauce, garlic powder, and cayenne, if using. Whisk until smooth and warm, then remove from the heat.

TOSS AND SERVE: In a large bowl, toss the hot, crispy wings with the warm buffalo sauce until well coated.

Serve immediately with ranch or blue cheese dressing, celery sticks, and plenty of napkins.

FLAVOR BOOST: When you pull that buffalo sauce off the heat, stir in a little grated parm. It melts right in, giving you a nutty creamy kick that'll have your guests thinking you're a culinary wizard.

Smoked Fried Lemon Garlic Wings

These Smoked Fried Lemon Garlic Flappers are lethal! Smoky, crispy, tangy, and loaded with enough garlic to take down Nosferatu himself. Lemon and garlic are the perfect tag team. These wings don't just smack . . . they bite back.

SERVES: 4 TO 6
PREP TIME: 15 MINUTES
MARINATE TIME: 4 HOURS OR OVERNIGHT
SMOKE TIME: 1 HOUR TO 1 HOUR 15 MINUTES
FRY TIME: 3 TO 4 MINUTES PER BATCH
TOTAL TIME (EXCLUDING MARINATING): ABOUT 1½ HOURS

WINGS AND MARINADE

2 pounds chicken party wings (about 20 pieces), separated into flats and drums

1 tablespoon kosher salt

1 teaspoon freshly ground black pepper

1 teaspoon garlic powder

Zest of 2 lemons

¼ cup freshly squeezed lemon juice

8 cloves garlic, finely grated or minced

1 tablespoon fish sauce

2 tablespoons extra-virgin olive oil

FOR SMOKING

Cherry, apple, or oak

DREDGING AND FRYING

1 cup cornstarch

1 cup all-purpose flour

2 teaspoons kosher salt

1 teaspoon garlic powder

6 to 8 cups neutral oil (enough to deep-fry)

LEMON-GARLIC SAUCE

4 tablespoons unsalted butter

6 cloves garlic, minced

2 tablespoons freshly squeezed lemon juice

1 teaspoon lemon zest

1 teaspoon fish sauce

GARNISH

¼ cup thinly sliced fresh basil leaves (chiffonade)

Red pepper flakes or lemon zest (optional)

MARINATE THE WINGS: In a large bowl, combine the chicken wings, salt, black pepper, garlic powder, lemon zest, lemon juice, garlic cloves, fish sauce, and olive oil. Toss well to coat, cover, and refrigerate for at least 4 hours, or overnight.

SMOKE THE WINGS: Preheat your smoker to 250°F. Remove the wings from the marinade and discard the marinade; place the wings directly on the smoker grates. Smoke for 60 to 75 minutes, or until the wings reach an internal temperature of 165°F and have a light golden exterior. Let cool slightly before frying.

DREDGE AND FRY: In a shallow bowl, mix the cornstarch, flour, salt, and garlic powder. Dredge the smoked wings until fully coated. Heat the neutral oil in a deep pot or fryer over medium-high heat to 350°F. Fry the wings in batches for 3 to 4 minutes until golden and crispy. Drain on a wire rack.

MAKE THE LEMON-GARLIC SAUCE: In a small saucepan over medium heat, melt the butter. Add the garlic cloves and sauté for 1 minute until fragrant. Stir in the lemon juice, lemon zest, and fish sauce. Cook for another minute.

TOSS, GARNISH, AND SERVE: In a large bowl, toss the hot, crispy wings in the lemon-garlic sauce until fully coated. Garnish with the basil and red pepper flakes, if using, or lemon zest. Serve immediately.

BOSS MOVE

Dip some lemon wedges in some chili salt and serve them alongside your wings for a colorful garnish that doubles as a build-your-own citrus-blast adventure.

Liquid Gold Chicken

In 2023, I competed on BBQ Brawl for Food Network. Before I left, I asked my daughter what her favorite thing I make is. She said, "Chicken." So, I brought the heat, and, thankfully, the judges felt the same. This is that dish: juicy, smoky, and glazed in buttery, golden goodness. Liquid gold, straight from the heart.

SERVES: 4 TO 6
PREP TIME: 20 MINUTES
COOK TIME: 1½ TO 2 HOURS

CHICKEN

One 4-to-5-pound whole chicken, spatchcocked or halved, or 4 bone-in, skin-on chicken breasts

2 tablespoons extra-virgin olive oil

SPG SANTA MARIA RUB

1½ tablespoons kosher salt

1 tablespoon freshly ground black pepper

2 teaspoons garlic powder

1 teaspoon onion powder (optional)

1 teaspoon dried parsley or oregano (optional—Santa Maria twist)

LIQUID GOLD INJECTION

½ cup unsalted butter, melted

¾ cup chicken broth

1½ teaspoons garlic powder

1 teaspoon MSG (or ½ teaspoon kosher salt, if omitting MSG)

FOR SMOKING

I like oak, red oak, or mesquite

PREP THE BIRD AND RUB: Pat the chicken dry with paper towels. Rub all over with the olive oil. In a small bowl, combine the salt, pepper, garlic powder, onion powder, if using, and dried parsley or oregano, if using. Season the chicken generously with this rub.

MAKE THE LIQUID GOLD INJECTION: In a small bowl, whisk together the melted butter, chicken broth, garlic powder, and MSG or salt.

INJECT THE CHICKEN: Using a meat injector, inject the liquid gold mixture into the thickest parts of the bird (breasts, thighs, and drumsticks, if using a whole chicken). Use about ½ cup total, distributing it evenly.

Cooking (choose your method):

SMOKER METHOD: Preheat your smoker to 325°F with a mild wood. Place the chicken skin-side up in the smoker and smoke for about 1 hour 20 minutes, or until the internal temperature is 155°F in the breast and 165°F in the thigh. To crisp the skin, flip your chicken to skin-side down and crank up the smoker to 400°F. Cook for another 10 minutes or so until the skin is crisp. Pull the chicken from the smoker at 160°F in the breast as it will continue to cook as it rests and hit 165°F internal temperature.

OVEN METHOD: Preheat the oven to 350°F. Place the chicken on a wire rack set in a roasting pan. Roast for about 1 hour 20 minutes, or until the internal temperature is 155°F in the breast and 165°F in the thigh. To crisp the skin, broil on high for 5 to 10 minutes (watching carefully to prevent burning) or sear skin-side down in a hot cast-iron skillet for a few minutes. Pull the chicken from the heat at 160°F in the breast, as it will continue to cook as it rests and will hit 165°F.

REST AND GARNISH: Let the chicken rest for 10 to 15 minutes before carving or serving. This chicken is finger lickin' on its own but also pairs well with Salsa Verde (page 145), Chimichurri (page 35), or Cali White Sauce (page 81).

BOSS MOVE

Once the chicken's rested, brush it with melted butter, a squeeze of lemon, and a hit of your rub. This is how you layer the flavor and do it major.

Cali White Sauce Wings

This is my West Coast remix of a Southern hit. I took Alabama's classic white sauce and gave it a Cali spin: amped up the herbs, cranked the tang, and made it way more fun. Game day, backyard hangs, or just because . . . these wings will have you California Dreamin'.

SERVES: 2 TO 4
PREP TIME: 30 MINUTES
SAUCE CHILL TIME: AT LEAST 30 MINUTES
ACTIVE COOK TIME (WINGS): 30 TO 40 MINUTES
TOTAL TIME (EXCLUDING SAUCE CHILL): ABOUT 60 MINUTES

CALI WHITE SAUCE

1 cup sour cream

1 cup Kewpie mayonnaise (or regular mayo)

4 tablespoons freshly squeezed lemon juice

2 tablespoons white wine vinegar

2 tablespoons extra-virgin olive oil

6 cloves garlic, finely minced

2 tablespoons chopped fresh cilantro (or parsley)

2 tablespoons chopped fresh chives

1 teaspoon kosher salt

1 teaspoon freshly ground black pepper

4 teaspoons finely minced jalapeño (seeds removed if you want less heat)

WINGS

2 pounds chicken wings (about 20 to 24 pieces, flats and drums)

3 tablespoons brown sugar

1½ tablespoons kosher salt

½ tablespoon smoked paprika

2 teaspoons garlic powder

2 teaspoons onion powder

1 teaspoon freshly ground black pepper

1 teaspoon Aleppo pepper (optional, for that Cali heat)

MAKE THE CALI WHITE SAUCE: In a medium bowl, whisk together the sour cream, mayo, lemon juice, white wine vinegar, and olive oil until smooth. Stir in the garlic, cilantro, chives, salt, black pepper, and minced jalapeño. Cover and refrigerate for at least 30 minutes so those flavors can meld and level up.

SEASON THE WINGS: In a small bowl, mix together the brown sugar, smoked paprika, garlic powder, onion powder, salt, black pepper, and Aleppo pepper (if using). Pat your chicken wings dry with paper towels, then toss and coat evenly with the seasoning blend until every piece is covered and ready to rock.

COOK THE WINGS (CHOOSE YOUR METHOD): Preheat your smoker, oven, or air fryer to 350°F. If baking or using an air fryer, be sure to place your wings in a single layer and not stack them on top of one another. Cook for 30 to 40 minutes, flipping halfway, or until the skin is golden, tight, and crisp. The internal temperature will likely exceed 165°F, that's okay for wings; crispy skin is the goal.

SERVE 'EM UP: Plate the hot, crispy wings and serve with your Cali white sauce, for drizzling, dunking, or smothering. Alternatively, you can dunk them in the sauce and throw them back on the heat for a few more minutes before finishing with more sauce.

BOSS MOVE

After saucing, hit 'em with toasted sesame seeds and some thin-sliced pickled red onions. The nutty sesame and tangy onions are the surprise duo you didn't even know you needed that adds a whole new meaning to "Cali fresh."

Lovely Lemon Rosemary Chicken

This one's personal. It's my take on my mom's rosemary chicken... the kind of dish that made the whole house smell like love. Bright lemon, crispy skin, and a pan sauce so good you'll wanna drink it. This is the type of dish I'd run home to eat after playing streetball to claim my seat at the table. It's simple, soulful, and meant to be shared with people you love.

SERVES: 4 TO 6

PREP TIME: 20 MINUTES

MARINATE TIME: AT LEAST 1 HOUR, PREFERABLY 4 TO 6 HOURS, OR OVERNIGHT

COOK TIME: 30 TO 50 MINUTES, DEPENDING ON METHOD

METHOD: GRILL/SMOKER OR OVEN

3 tablespoons extra-virgin olive oil, divided

Zest and juice of 1 lemon

6 cloves garlic, minced

1 tablespoon fresh rosemary, finely chopped, or 1½ teaspoons dried

1 teaspoon Dijon mustard

1 tablespoon kosher salt

½ tablespoon freshly ground black pepper

½ teaspoon red pepper flakes (optional)

2 pounds bone-in, skin-on chicken thighs (4 to 6 pieces)

½ cup chicken broth

Lemon slices and fresh rosemary sprigs, for garnish

MARINATE THE CHICKEN: In a bowl, whisk together 2 tablespoons of the olive oil, the lemon zest, lemon juice, minced garlic, chopped rosemary, Dijon mustard, salt, black pepper, and red pepper flakes, if using. Place the chicken thighs in a large resealable bag or shallow dish and pour the marinade over them. Ensure the chicken is well coated. Marinate in the refrigerator for at least 1 hour, preferably 4 to 6 hours or overnight for maximum flavor.

SEAR THE CHICKEN (CHOOSE YOUR METHOD):

GRILL OPTION: Preheat a charcoal grill to medium-high heat. Place the chicken thighs skin-side down over direct heat and sear for 5 to 7 minutes until the skin is crisp and golden.

CAST-IRON SKILLET OPTION: Preheat a cast-iron skillet over medium-high heat with the remaining 1 tablespoon olive oil. Place the chicken thighs skin-side down in the skillet and sear for 5 to 7 minutes until the skin is crisp and golden.

FINISH COOKING (CHOOSE YOUR METHOD):

GRILL/SMOKER METHOD: Preheat your smoker or grill to 350°F (indirect heat). Transfer the seared chicken thighs to a grill-safe pan or cast-iron skillet, skin-side up. Pour the chicken broth into the pan, avoiding pouring it over the skin to maintain its crispiness. Place the lemon slices and rosemary sprigs around the chicken. Cover the pan with foil and cook in the smoker or on the indirect side of the grill for 20 to 25 minutes, or until the internal temperature reaches 175°F.

OVEN METHOD: Preheat your oven to 400°F. After searing, transfer the chicken thighs to an oven-safe dish, skin-side up. Pour the chicken broth into the dish, avoiding pouring it over the skin. Place the lemon slices and rosemary sprigs around the chicken. Cover with foil and bake for 35 to 45 minutes, or until the internal temperature reaches 175°F.

SERVE: Let the chicken rest for 5 minutes before serving. Garnish with the cooked lemon slices and rosemary sprigs. Serve with mashed or roasted potatoes, grilled vegetables, or a fresh salad.

FLAVOR BOOST: Right before serving, spoon a little of that lemony pan juice over the chicken, along with a fresh grating of lemon zest and a tiny drizzle of olive oil. Serve it with charred lemons and watch folks lick their plates clean.

4.6% ALC/VOL

Sweet Heat Sriracha Sando

This sandwich goes full send!! Crispy buttermilk-fried chicken glazed in sticky-sweet sriracha, piled high on a brioche bun with tangy Asian slaw. BIG FLAVOR! BIG CRUNCH! BIG MESS!! Grab a napkin and let it wreck your day in the best way!

SERVES: 4
PREP TIME: 20 MINUTES
MARINATE TIME: AT LEAST 1 HOUR OR OVERNIGHT
COOK TIME: 30 MINUTES

CHICKEN AND MARINADE

1 cup buttermilk

1 egg

2 tablespoons sriracha

1 tablespoon honey

1 teaspoon garlic powder

1 teaspoon kosher salt

½ teaspoon freshly ground black pepper

4 boneless, skinless chicken thighs or breasts, pounded to ½-inch thickness

SWEET SRIRACHA GLAZE

¼ cup honey

2 tablespoons sriracha

1 tablespoon soy sauce

1 tablespoon rice vinegar

1 teaspoon unsalted butter

TANGY ASIAN SLAW

One 14-to-16 ounce bag cabbage-and-carrot coleslaw mix

2 green onions, whites and green parts, thinly sliced

¼ cup chopped fresh cilantro

DRESSING

¼ cup rice vinegar

1 tablespoon soy sauce

1 tablespoon sesame oil

2 teaspoons sugar or honey

1 teaspoon sriracha (for heat, optional)

Juice of ½ lime

Pinch of kosher salt and freshly ground black pepper

1 tablespoon mayonnaise (optional)

DREDGE AND FOR FRYING

1½ cups all-purpose flour

½ cup cornstarch

2 tablespoons BBQ rub

Neutral oil (canola or vegetable)

FOR ASSEMBLY

4 brioche buns

Mayonnaise or aioli of choice (garlic, lemon, and wasabi work great)

MARINATE THE CHICKEN: In a bowl or zip-top bag, whisk together the buttermilk, egg, sriracha, honey, garlic powder, salt, and pepper. Add the chicken thighs (or breasts) to the mixture. Toss to coat and marinate in the fridge for at least 1 hour, or overnight for maximum flavor.

MAKE THE SWEET SRIRACHA GLAZE: In a small saucepan over medium heat, combine the honey, sriracha, soy sauce, vinegar, and butter. Simmer for 3 to 5 minutes, stirring, until slightly thick and glossy. Set aside.

MAKE THE TANGY ASIAN SLAW: In a large mixing bowl, combine the coleslaw mix, green onions, and cilantro. To make the dressing: in a small bowl, whisk together the vinegar, soy sauce, sesame oil, sugar or honey, sriracha, if using, lime juice, salt, pepper to taste and mayo, if using. Pour the dressing over the slaw and toss well. Let the mixture sit for 10 to 15 minutes while everything else cooks.

DREDGE AND FRY THE CHICKEN: In a shallow dish, mix together the flour, cornstarch, and rub. Heat 1 to 2 inches of oil in a cast-iron skillet over medium-high heat or deep fryer to 350°F. Remove each piece of chicken from the marinade, letting the excess drip off. Press firmly into the seasoned flour mixture until evenly coated.

Fry in batches for 5 to 6 minutes per side, or until golden brown and the internal temperature reaches 165°F. Drain on a wire rack.

GLAZE AND BUILD THE SANDWICH: While the chicken is still hot, brush or toss each piece with the sweet sriracha glaze. Toast the buns. Spread the bottom buns with your choice of mayo or aioli. Build each sandwich: bottom bun, glazed fried chicken, a scoop of slaw, more glaze, if you'd like, and the top bun.

BOSS MOVE

Fresh out the fryer, hit that chicken with flaky salt so the glaze sticks and the flavor blasts off. Stack the sandwich, then hit the slaw with a squeeze of lime and a sprinkle of sesame seeds to unlock new levels of flavor.

Smoked Chicken con Queso

This one's the ultimate munchie move. Smoky, cheesy, melty goodness piled high and stupid easy to throw together. Fun to make whether you're feeding the kids or the whole squad on game day. Tender smoked chicken folded into gooey queso... it's messy, bold, and so good you'll be dipping back nonstop.

SERVES: 4 TO 6
PREP TIME: 15 MINUTES
SMOKE TIME (CHICKEN): 45 TO 60 MINUTES
BRAISE TIME: 30 MINUTES
FINISH SMOKE TIME (QUESO): 15 TO 20 MINUTES
TOTAL TIME: 1½ TO 2 HOURS

TACO SEASONING (OR A STANDARD PACKET OF YOUR FAVORITE TACO SEASONING)

1 tablespoon good-quality chili powder

1½ teaspoons smoked paprika (Spanish sweet or bittersweet)

2 teaspoons ground cumin

1½ teaspoons garlic powder

1½ teaspoons onion powder

1 teaspoon dried Mexican oregano or regular oregano

1 teaspoon kosher salt

¾ teaspoon freshly ground black pepper

¾ teaspoon ground coriander

¼ to ½ teaspoon cayenne pepper (adjust to your heat preference)

¼ teaspoon chipotle powder (optional flavor booster)

1½ to 2 pounds boneless, skinless chicken thighs

1 cup chicken broth

One 4-ounce can chopped green chiles, drained

1 cup chunky salsa

1 cup cream cheese

2 cups shredded Monterey Jack cheese, Colby Jack, or Mexican blend

¼ cup sour cream

1 bunch cilantro, finely minced (about ½ cup)

FOR SMOKING

Hickory, oak, or pecan

PREPARE THE TACO SEASONING AND SEASON CHICKEN: In a small bowl, thoroughly mix all the ingredients for the homemade taco seasoning. Rub your taco seasoning mix generously all over the chicken thighs, ensuring even coverage. Use the full amount of seasoning.

SMOKE THE CHICKEN: Preheat your smoker to 250°F. Place the seasoned chicken thighs directly on the smoker grates. Smoke for 45 to 60 minutes, or until the chicken reaches an internal temperature of 160°F to 165°F and has taken on a nice smoky color.

BRAISE TO TENDERIZE: Transfer the smoked chicken thighs into a disposable foil pan (or an oven-safe dish). Pour the chicken broth into the pan around the chicken. Cover the pan tightly with heavy-duty aluminum foil. Return the covered pan to the smoker. Increase the smoker temperature to 300°F. Braise for 30 minutes, or until the chicken is very tender and shreds easily with a fork.

SHRED AND COMBINE: Carefully remove the pan from the smoker (be cautious of hot steam when uncovering). Using two forks or gloved hands, shred the braised chicken right in the pan, incorporating it with the braising liquids.

To the shredded chicken, add: the green chilies, salsa, cream cheese, Monterey Jack cheese, sour cream, and cilantro. Stir everything together until well mixed and all the chicken is coated in the cheesy, saucy mixture.

SMOKE TO FINISH: Leave the pan uncovered. Return it to the smoker (still at 300°F) for 15 to 20 minutes. Cook until the cheese is fully melted, bubbly, and perhaps slightly golden brown around the edges.

SERVE IT UP: Let it cool for a few minutes as it will be very hot. Spoon the smoked chicken con queso into warm tacos, load it into burritos, pile it high on nachos or fries, or simply serve it in a bowl with tortilla chips for dipping. This one's rich, smoky, and unapologetically cheesy.

BOSS MOVE

When the queso's bubbly and melty, toss on more cheese and let it ride 5 minutes to get that golden crust. Right before serving, hit it with a drizzle of hot sauce, a squeeze of lime juice, and a shower of fresh cilantro.

Chicken Caprese Grilled Cheese

SERVES: 2
PREP TIME: 10 MINUTES
COOK TIME: 20 MINUTES
TOTAL TIME: 30 MINUTES

As a kid, grilled cheese felt like the peak. Then I went and stuffed mine with chicken, melty mozz, tomatoes, and basil . . . I quickly realized I had changed the game. It's easy, cheesy, and over the top. Fresh AF and perfect for lunch, dinner, or that midnight fridge raid.

CHICKEN

- 2 boneless, skinless chicken breasts (1¼ to 1½ pounds total), pounded to ½-inch thickness
- 1 tablespoon extra-virgin olive oil, plus more for grilling
- 1 teaspoon kosher salt
- ½ teaspoon freshly ground black pepper
- 1 teaspoon garlic powder
- 1 teaspoon Italian seasoning

SANDWICH BUILD

- 1 tablespoon mayonnaise
- 1 tablespoon unsalted butter, at room temperature
- 4 slices thick sourdough or artisan white bread (¾-inch thick)
- 2 tablespoons pesto (store-bought or homemade)
- ½ cup shredded, low-moisture mozzarella cheese
- 4 slices fresh mozzarella cheese (2 ounces)
- 4 to 6 slices ripe tomato (¼-inch thick)
- 8 to 12 fresh basil leaves
- 4 teaspoons balsamic glaze

SEASON AND COOK THE CHICKEN: Rub the chicken breasts with the olive oil. Season all sides evenly with the salt, black pepper, garlic powder, and Italian seasoning. Heat your griddle or a large skillet to medium-high heat (around 375°F). Add a little oil to the surface.

Place the chicken on the hot surface and cook for 3 to 4 minutes per side, until golden with slight char and the internal temperature reaches 165°F. Rest the chicken for 5 minutes, then slice thinly.

PREP THE BREAD: In a small bowl, stir together the mayo and butter. Spread this blend on the *outside* of each bread slice. On the *inside* of two slices of bread, smear 1 tablespoon pesto.

BUILD THE MELT (PER SANDWICH): On the pesto-smeared side of each of the two bread slices, layer ¼ cup shredded mozzarella, half of the sliced cooked chicken, 2 slices of fresh mozzarella, 2 or 3 tomato slices, 4 to 6 basil leaves, and 2 teaspoons balsamic glaze. Cap with the second slice of bread (buttered/mayo-side out).

GRILL THE SANDWICH: Clean off your griddle or skillet, then heat to medium (325°F to 350°F). Place the sandwiches on the griddle and press gently with a spatula. Cook for 3 to 4 minutes per side, until golden brown and crisp. You can cover with a melting dome or a metal bowl for the last 2 minutes of cooking to ensure the cheese is fully melted.

SERVE IT UP: Slice diagonally to show off the melt. Serve with a side of extra pesto or balsamic glaze for dipping (optional).

BOSS MOVE

Before you build, toss that sliced chicken in olive oil and a spoonful of pesto and let it soak up the extra flavor. Hit it with flaky salt and a little garlic butter, then stack it up. Next. Level. Delicious.

Chicken Continental

This isn't just chicken and rice; it's a creamy, dreamy hug in a casserole dish, straight from the heart of home cooking. We're talking tender chicken nestled in a ridiculously rich, savory rice bath, boosted with secret umami weapons. My mom would make this, and it warmed my soul every time. I hope my version does the same for you.

SERVES: 4
PREP TIME: 10 MINUTES
COOK TIME: ABOUT 1 HOUR

- 4 boneless, skinless chicken thighs (or drums and even breasts)
- Kosher salt and freshly ground black pepper
- 1 to 2 tablespoons extra-virgin olive oil or unsalted butter, plus more as needed
- 6 cloves garlic, minced
- ½ pound mushrooms, sliced thin (optional, but do it)
- One 10½-ounce can cream of mushroom soup
- One 10½-ounce can cream of chicken soup
- 1¾ cups chicken broth
- 1½ tablespoons white miso paste
- 1 tablespoon Worcestershire sauce
- 1 teaspoon onion powder
- ½ teaspoon paprika
- 1¼ cups long-grain white rice
- 1 tablespoon chopped fresh parsley, for garnish (optional)

PREHEAT THE OVEN AND PREP CHICKEN: Preheat your oven to 350°F. Pat the chicken dry and lightly season it with salt and pepper. Heat 1 tablespoon of the olive oil or butter in a skillet over medium-high heat. Sear the chicken in the hot oil for 2 to 3 minutes per side just to build some color and flavor. Set aside (it will not be cooked through).

Add more olive oil to the pan if needed. Add the garlic and cook for 1 minute or until fragrant. Add the mushrooms, if using. Sauté the mushroom-garlic mixture for 3 to 5 minutes until just softened but not cooked through. Remove from the heat.

MIX THE BASE: In a large bowl, combine the cream of mushroom soup, cream of chicken soup, chicken broth, white miso paste, Worcestershire sauce, onion powder, pepper, and paprika. Stir well until smooth and the miso is fully incorporated.

ASSEMBLE THE DISH: In a 9-inch-by-13-inch baking dish, spread the rice evenly. Pour in the soup mixture and then scatter the sautéed mushrooms, if using, over the rice and stir gently to combine and ensure the rice is submerged. Nestle the seared chicken pieces on top of the rice mixture.

BAKE COVERED: Cover the baking dish tightly with foil. Bake for 45 minutes.

BAKE UNCOVERED: Remove the foil and bake for another 15 to 20 minutes, or until the rice is tender and most of the liquid has been absorbed, the remaining sauce is bubbling, and the chicken is firm to the touch (it will likely be above 165°F internal as well). If desired, you can broil for the last 2 minutes to brown the top slightly, watching carefully to prevent burning.

REST AND SERVE: Let the dish sit for 5 to 10 minutes after removing from the oven. Season to taste if needed. Garnish with the chopped fresh parsley, if using, and serve.

BOSS MOVE

About 5 minutes before it's done baking, shower the top with a big handful of crispy fried onions. They take this creamy dish straight into the comfort food hall of fame with even more texture and flavor!

CHAPTER 3

PORK

THE HOG LINE

Welcome to the Hog Line, where pork is king and the flavor don't quit. This is the part of the ride where we get messy, bold, and a little bit wild. We're throwing down sticky shanks that fall apart in your hands, juicy chops that are layered with flavor, tender belly that melts in your mouth, and pulled pork so tender it might make you cry a little. Every recipe in here brings that sweet, smoky, salty magic that only pork can deliver. Big bites, big energy, and zero apologies. Let's go full hog and get hyphy!

Shreds Like Butter!

Teriyaki Pork Belly Bombs

These Teriyaki Pork Belly Bombs blew up for a reason. They're as addictive as your favorite playlist on repeat. Crispy, sticky, sweet, and savory, you can crush 'em any way you like: over rice, stuffed in tacos, or straight from the tray. Just know they'll be gone before you blink, so double up.

SERVES: 6 TO 8 AS AN APPETIZER
PREP TIME: 15 MINUTES
COOK TIME: ABOUT 3 HOURS 45 MINUTES
TOTAL TIME: ABOUT 4 HOURS

PORK BELLY

One 3-to-4-pound slab pork belly, skin removed

3 tablespoons of your favorite BBQ rub or seasoning blend

HOMEMADE TERIYAKI SAUCE

½ cup soy sauce

3 tablespoons honey

¼ cup packed brown sugar

3 tablespoons fresh grated ginger, or 1 tablespoon ground ginger

3 tablespoons garlic powder or 2 tablespoons minced garlic

SLURRY

¼ cup cornstarch mixed with ¼ cup cold water

PREPARE AND SMOKE THE PORK BELLY: Cut the pork belly into 1-inch cubes. Season the cubes evenly with the rub. Preheat your smoker to 250°F. Place the pork belly cubes directly on the smoker grates or on a wire rack. Smoke for 1½ to 2 hours, or until a deep mahogany bark has formed and the rub has set.

MAKE THE TERIYAKI SAUCE: While the pork belly smokes, combine 1 cup water, the soy sauce, honey, brown sugar, grated ginger, and garlic powder in a saucepan. Bring to a gentle boil over medium-high heat. If short on time, store-bought teriyaki sauce can be used, but homemade offers a superior flavor.

Stir in the cornstarch slurry. Reduce the heat to low and simmer for 5 to 10 minutes, stirring frequently, until the sauce has thickened. Remove from the heat and set aside.

BRAISE THE PORK BELLY: Transfer the smoked pork belly cubes into a foil pan in a single layer. Cover the pan tightly with foil. Return to the smoker (still at 250°F) and braise for 1½ hours to tenderize.

GLAZE AND FINISH: After braising, carefully remove the foil from the pan and pour off any excess rendered fat. Pour 1 to 1½ cups of the homemade teriyaki sauce over the pork bites, just enough to coat them well. Toss the pork bites gently to ensure they are evenly coated in the sauce. Return the uncovered pan to the smoker for 20 to 30 minutes to allow the glaze to set and caramelize slightly.

SERVE: Let the pork belly bites rest for 5 to 10 minutes. Serve hot.

BOSS MOVE

Right before the final glaze, press those bites down a little with a spatula to open up more surface for the sauce to stick and to build that crispy caramelized edge in the smoker. After glazing, finish with fresh lime zest and a sprinkle of toasted sesame seeds for deliciousness that's hard to describe.

Mango Pig Wings

Pig wings don't fly, but trust me, they vanish quickly. Juicy pork shanks get hit with a tropical mango glaze that's sticky, sweet, and packed with flavor. Every bite is rich, messy in the best way, and addictive enough to have you licking your fingers clean. It's a wild cut, but once you try it, you'll be hooked.

SERVES: 4 AS AN APPETIZER
PREP TIME: 15 MINUTES
SMOKE TIME: 1½ TO 2 HOURS
BRAISE TIME: 1 TO 1½ HOURS
GLAZE TIME: 15 TO 20 MINUTES
TOTAL COOK TIME: 3 TO 4 HOURS

PIG WINGS

8 pork shanks (a.k.a. pig wings, 4 to 5 pounds total)

2 tablespoons yellow mustard (binder)

3 tablespoons BBQ rub (sweet-and-smoky style recommended)

BRAISE

½ cup mango nectar

4 tablespoons unsalted butter, divided

MANGO GLAZE

1 cup mango nectar

2 tablespoons honey

1 tablespoon rice vinegar or apple cider vinegar

1 tablespoon soy sauce

1 tablespoon freshly squeezed lime juice

1 teaspoon red pepper flakes (optional)

½ teaspoon garlic powder

Pinch of salt

FOR SMOKING

Mild fruitwood like cherry or apple

PREP THE PIG WINGS: Pat the pork shanks dry with paper towels. Rub them all over with the yellow mustard. Season generously on all sides with the rub. Let sit at room temperature while the smoker heats up.

SMOKE: Preheat your smoker to 275°F. Place pig wings directly on the smoker grate. Smoke for 1½ to 2 hours, flipping once halfway through. You're looking for rich color and slight bark formation.

BRAISE: For each shank, lay out a piece of heavy-duty foil. Place a shank in the center, top with ½ tablespoon of butter and drizzle with 1 tablespoon of mango nectar. Wrap each shank tightly in its foil packet. Return the wrapped shanks to the smoker (or transfer to a 300°F oven). Braise for 1 to 1½ hours, until the internal temperature is 195°F to 200°F and the meat is tender.

MAKE THE MANGO GLAZE: While the pig wings braise, combine all the glaze ingredients in a small saucepan. Bring to a simmer over medium heat and cook for 10 to 15 minutes, stirring occasionally, until the glaze is thick and glossy.

GLAZE AND FINISH: Carefully unwrap the braised shanks from the foil (reserve any juices for another use or discard). Brush the shanks generously with the mango glaze or dunk them if the glaze is in a suitable container. Return the glazed shanks, unwrapped, to the smoker or grill (direct medium heat) for 15 to 20 minutes to caramelize the glaze.

SERVE: Let the pig wings rest for 5 minutes before serving. Garnish with chopped fresh cilantro or sliced green onions, if desired. Serve any extra glaze on the side.

FLAVOR BOOST: Right before serving, shower those glazed pig wings with toasted coconut flakes and a hit of fresh lime zest. You add the lime and the coconut and you'll want to eat 'em all up.

Mojo Pork Booty

My wife is Cuban, so mojo is basically in my blood now, and this mojo pork booty is a tribute to that flavor. Juicy, garlicky, tangy, and ridiculously easy to make, it's the kind of dish that disappears fast and keeps everyone coming back for more. Skip the basic pulled pork. Smoke this instead.

SERVES: 8+
PREP TIME: 25 MINUTES
MARINATE TIME: 4 TO 12 HOURS, PREFERABLY OVERNIGHT
SMOKE TIME: 6 TO 8 HOURS
REST TIME: AT LEAST 1 HOUR
TOTAL TIME (EXCLUDING MARINATING): 7 TO 9 HOURS

MOJO MARINADE

1½ cups freshly squeezed orange juice

¾ cup freshly squeezed lime juice

½ cup olive oil

2 tablespoons soy sauce

1 tablespoon white vinegar

10 cloves garlic, smashed

1 small bunch cilantro (stems and leaves), coarsely chopped

1 jalapeño, halved (optional, for mild heat)

Zest of 1 orange

Zest of 1 lime (reserve the lime for squeezing over the finished pork)

2 teaspoons kosher salt, plus more as needed

PORK

One 4-to-5-pound boneless pork shoulder (Boston butt)

DRY RUB

1 tablespoon kosher salt

1 tablespoon freshly ground black pepper

1 tablespoon garlic powder

1 tablespoon ground cumin

2 teaspoons smoked paprika

1 teaspoon dried oregano

½ teaspoon ground cloves (optional, but recommended)

MARINATE THE PORK: In a blender, combine all the marinade ingredients. Blend until smooth. Taste and adjust the salt if needed.

Score the fat cap of the pork shoulder in a crosshatch pattern, about ¼ inch deep. Place the pork in a large zip-top bag, a non-reactive deep container, or a vacuum-seal bag. Pour about two-thirds of the marinade over the pork, ensuring it's well coated. Reserve the remaining marinade in the refrigerator for basting and finishing the sauce. Marinate in the refrigerator for at least 4 hours, but preferably overnight (up to 12 hours).

Remove the pork from the marinade, discarding the used marinade. Pat t he pork mostly dry with paper towels. In a small bowl, mix together all the dry rub seasonings. Coat the pork shoulder generously and evenly with the dry rub.

Preheat your smoker to 250°F. Place the pork shoulder fat-side up on the smoker grates. Smoke for 4 to 5 hours, or until the internal temperature reaches 165°F and a good bark has formed. You can baste with some of the reserved (unused) marinade every hour or so if desired.

WRAP AND FINISH: Remove the pork from the smoker. Wrap it tightly in butcher paper or heavy-duty aluminum foil. If using foil, add a little of the reserved marinade before sealing. Return the wrapped pork to the smoker and continue cooking until it reaches an internal temperature of 203°F and is probe-tender. This can take another 2 to 4 hours.

REST, SAUCE, AND SHRED: Remove the pork remove it from the smoker and vent it to let it rest at room temperature for 15 minutes before covering and placing in a cooler or an oven on the warm setting, for at least one hour, or up to 2 hours.

While the pork rests, gently simmer the reserved (unused) mojo marinade in a small saucepan for 5 to 10 minutes over medium heat until slightly thickened. After resting, unwrap the pork (reserve any accumulated juices) and shred it using two forks or meat claws. Mix some of the warm mojo sauce and any reserved pork juices into the shredded pork. Taste and adjust the seasoning, adding more salt or a squeeze of fresh lime juice for brightness if needed.

BOSS MOVE

For extra texture, crisp some shredded pork under the broiler or in a hot skillet with a little mojo till the edges brown up. Mojo carnitas!!! Perfect for tacos, bowls, or Cuban sandwiches.

Balsamic Pork Belly

I wanted to make something different, something that makes people say "wow," while still shouting out my Italian dad and where I grew up. These Italian Balsamic Pork Belly Pops do just that. Serve 'em on a stick, hit 'em with a cheese shower and fresh herbs, and you're the appetizer MVP.

SERVES: 4 TO 6 AS AN APPETIZER
PREP TIME: 20 MINUTES
MARINATE TIME: AT LEAST 1 HOUR, OR OVERNIGHT
COOK TIME: 3 TO 3½ HOURS

PORK BELLY

One 3-to-4-pound slab skinless pork belly

2 tablespoons olive oil

1 tablespoon balsamic vinegar

1 tablespoon freshly squeezed lemon juice

2 teaspoons garlic powder

2 teaspoons fennel seed, lightly crushed

1 teaspoon dried oregano

1 teaspoon fresh rosemary, finely chopped, or ½ teaspoon dried rosemary

1½ teaspoons kosher salt

1 teaspoon freshly ground black pepper

Pinch of red pepper flakes (optional, for a touch of heat)

BRAISING LIQUID (OPTIONAL)

¼ cup chicken broth or dry white wine

GLAZE

½ cup balsamic vinegar

¼ cup honey

2 tablespoons brown sugar

1 tablespoon Dijon mustard

2 cloves garlic, finely minced

1 teaspoon finely chopped fresh rosemary

Pinch of salt

GARNISH

Grated Parmigiano-Reggiano cheese

Fresh parsley or basil, chopped

Drizzle of glaze or reduced balsamic vinegar (optional)

PREP AND MARINATE THE BELLY: Slice the pork belly into roughly 3-by-1-inch logs. In a large bowl, combine the olive oil, balsamic vinegar, lemon juice, garlic powder, fennel seed, dried oregano, rosemary, salt, black pepper, and red pepper flakes (if using).

Add the pork belly cubes to the marinade and toss to coat well. Cover and marinate in the refrigerator for at least 1 hour, or overnight for maximum flavor.

SMOKE OR ROAST: Preheat your smoker or oven to 275°F. Skewer the marinated pork pieces and place them on a wire rack set over a foil-lined tray (to catch drippings) or directly on the smoker grates. Smoke/roast for 2 to 2½ hours, until the bark has set and some fat has rendered.

WRAP AND BRAISE: Transfer the pork cubes to a foil pan. If desired, add the chicken broth or white wine to the pan. Cover the pan tightly with foil and return to the smoker/oven for another 45 minutes to 1 hour to soften and tenderize further.

MAKE THE GLAZE: While the pork is braising (or toward the end of the initial smoke/roast), prepare the glaze. In a small saucepan, combine the balsamic vinegar, honey, brown sugar, Dijon mustard, garlic cloves, rosemary, and salt. Bring to a simmer over medium heat and cook for 10 to 12 minutes, stirring occasionally, until the glaze is syrupy and glossy.

GLAZE AND CARAMELIZE: If you braised the pork, carefully remove it from the foil pan, discarding excess liquid. Brush them generously with the balsamic glaze. Increase your smoker/oven to 300°F to 325°F. Return the lollipops (uncovered) to the heat for 15 to 20 minutes, brushing once or twice more with glaze, until they're glossy and candied. Watch closely to prevent burning.

GARNISH AND SERVE: Pull them from the heat and let them rest for 2 to 3 minutes. Immediately dust them with grated Parmigiano-Reggiano so it melts slightly into the glaze while they're still hot. Finish with fresh parsley or basil, and an optional drizzle of extra glaze or reduced balsamic vinegar. That little makes 'em pop and takes 'em over the top.

BOSS MOVE

Right before serving, drizzle those lollipops with chili hot honey. That sweet heat mixed with the balsamic glaze?!?! Ohweeee!!!

The Vineyard Tenderloin

This pork tenderloin is my love letter to Napa. Juicy off the grill, dripping with garlicky herb butter, and topped with sweet-blistered grapes that taste like vineyard sunshine. It's got smoky BBQ soul with a wine-country twist. Easy to make, crazy good to eat, and impossible not to love.

SERVES: 2 TO 3
PREP TIME: 10 MINUTES
MARINATE TIME: AT LEAST 15 MINUTES (WHILE THE GRILL HEATS) AND UP TO 2 HOURS
COOK TIME: 15 TO 20 MINUTES (PORK) PLUS 5 TO 7 MINUTES (GRAPES)
REST TIME (PORK): 10 MINUTES

PORK TENDERLOIN

1 tablespoon olive oil

1½ teaspoons Dijon mustard

1 teaspoon balsamic vinegar

1 teaspoon kosher salt

½ teaspoon freshly ground black pepper

½ teaspoon garlic powder

½ teaspoon fresh thyme, chopped, or a pinch of dried thyme

¼ teaspoon red pepper flakes

1 to 1¼ pounds pork tenderloin, trimmed of silver skin

BLISTERED GRAPES

1 heaping cup red or black seedless grapes

2 teaspoons olive oil

Pinch of flaky salt

Splash of balsamic vinegar (≠≠optional)

GARLIC-HERB BUTTER

2 tablespoons unsalted butter

1 clove garlic, minced

½ teaspoon chopped fresh rosemary

½ teaspoon chopped fresh thyme

Zest of ½ lemon

Kosher salt

MARINATE THE TENDERLOIN: In a small bowl, together the olive oil, Dijon mustard, balsamic vinegar, kosher salt, black pepper, garlic powder, thyme, and red pepper flakes. Rub this mixture all over the pork tenderloin. Let it marinate at room temperature while your grill heats up (at least 15 minutes) or cover and refrigerate for up to 2 hours.

GRILL THE PORK: Preheat your grill to medium-high heat. Grill the pork tenderloin, turning every 3 to 4 minutes to develop an even color and crust, for 12 to 18 minutes total, or until the internal temperature reaches 140°F to 145°F for medium and the pork is slightly pink.

Remove from the grill, tent loosely with foil, and let rest for 10 minutes. The temperature will continue to rise slightly.

BLISTER THE GRAPES: While the pork rests, heat a cast-iron pan or grill-safe skillet over high heat. Toss the grapes with the olive oil and a pinch of flaky salt. Add the grapes to the hot pan and cook, stirring occasionally, until they start to soften, pop, and char in spots, 5 to 7 minutes. If desired, splash with a little balsamic vinegar to deglaze the pan and coat the grapes.

MAKE THE GARLIC-HERB BUTTER: In a small saucepan or skillet, melt the butter over low heat. Add the garlic clove, rosemary, and thyme. Let the mixture sizzle gently for 1 to 2 minutes until fragrant, being careful not to burn the garlic. Remove from the heat and stir in the lemon zest and a pinch of salt, to taste.

SERVE IT UP: Slice the rested pork tenderloin against the grain into medallions. Arrange the pork slices on plates, accompany with the juicy blistered grapes, and spoon a generous amount of the garlic-herb butter over the top of the pork. Finish with an extra pinch of flaky salt, if desired.

BOSS MOVE

Right before serving, toss some crumbled blue cheese or Gorgonzola over the hot pork. That funky, creamy bite melts right into the grapes and herb butter like they were meant to be together.

Port 'n' Pork Sando

This port wine pork sandwich is the dream team of two of my favorites: port wine and BBQ. The rich, sweet port soaks into juicy pork, caramelized onions bring that melt-in-your-mouth magic, and the whole thing is a showstopper!

SERVES: 4

BRINE TIME: 3 TO 4 HOURS, OR OVERNIGHT

SMOKE TIME (PORK): 1½ TO 2 HOURS

REST TIME (PORK): 10 MINUTES

ONION AND AIOLI PREP: ABOUT 20 MINUTES

TOTAL TIME (EXCLUDING BRINE): ABOUT 2 TO 2½ HOURS

BRINE

¼ cup kosher salt

2 tablespoons brown sugar

1 tablespoon freshly ground black pepper

3 cloves garlic, smashed

1 sprig fresh rosemary or thyme (optional)

PORK LOIN

1½ to 2 pounds boneless pork loin (not tenderloin)

RUB (AFTER BRINING)

1 tablespoon olive oil

1 teaspoon garlic powder

1 teaspoon freshly ground black pepper

½ teaspoon smoked paprika

PORT WINE ONIONS

1 tablespoon unsalted butter or olive oil

2 red onions, thinly sliced

Pinch of kosher salt

½ cup ruby port wine

MUSTARD AIOLI

½ cup mayonnaise

2 tablespoons Dijon mustard

1 clove garlic, finely grated or minced

1 teaspoon freshly squeezed lemon juice

Pinch of salt

1 teaspoon whole-grain mustard (optional)

FOR ASSEMBLY

4 sturdy sandwich rolls or ciabatta buns

2 slices aged white cheddar or provolone cheese (optional)

1½ cups arugula or watercress

BRINE THE PORK LOIN: In a pot, combine 4 cups water, the salt, brown sugar, black pepper, garlic cloves, and 1 sprig rosemary or thyme, if using. Bring to a simmer, stirring to dissolve the salt and sugar. Remove from the heat and let cool completely.

Submerge the pork loin in the cooled brine. Cover and refrigerate for at least 3 hours, or ideally overnight.

SMOKE THE PORK LOIN: Remove the pork loin from the brine and discard the brine. Pat it thoroughly dry with paper towels. Rub the pork loin with the olive oil, then season evenly with the garlic powder, pepper, and smoked paprika.

Preheat your smoker to 250°F. Smoke the pork loin until the internal temperature reaches 140°F. This should take 1½ to 2 hours, depending on the thickness of the loin.

Remove the loin from the smoker, tent loosely with foil, and let rest for 10 minutes before slicing. The temperature will rise to about 145°F. Slice thinly against the grain.

MAKE THE PORTWINE ONIONS: While the pork smokes or rests, melt the butter in a pan over medium heat. Add the onions and a pinch of salt. Cook, stirring occasionally, for 10 to 12 minutes, until the onions are soft and slightly caramelized. Add the ruby port wine to the pan. Bring to a simmer and cook for 5 to 7 minutes, or until the liquid has reduced and become syrupy. Set aside.

MAKE THE MUSTARD AIOLI: In a small bowl, whisk together the mayonnaise, Dijon mustard, garlic clove, lemon juice, and a pinch of salt until smooth. Stir in the whole-grain mustard, if using. Set aside.

ASSEMBLE THE SANDWICHES: Split and toast the sandwich rolls or ciabatta buns. Spread a generous layer of mustard aioli on both cut sides of the toasted buns. Layer the sandwiches with thin slices of smoked pork loin, a spoonful of the port wine onions, a slice of cheese, if using, and a handful of arugula or watercress.

Place the top bun on and serve warm.

FLAVOR BOOST: Spread some whipped goat cheese and garlic aioli on the bun before stacking. That creamy layer balances the sweetness of the port onions and makes the whole sandwich hit just right.

Grilled Lemon Pepper Pork Piccata

Piccata's a classic and one of my favorites, so I gave it the BBQ spin. Fire-grilled pork chops seasoned up and drowned in buttery, garlicky piccata sauce with wine, capers, and lemon. Crazy easy to make and the perfect elevated Italian twist on BBQ. The ultimate weeknight wonder.

SERVES: 4
BRINE TIME (OPTIONAL): 1 HOUR
PREP TIME: 15 MINUTES
COOK TIME: 20 MINUTES
TOTAL TIME (EXCLUDING OPTIONAL BRINE): 30 MINUTES

QUICK BRINE (OPTIONAL)

3 tablespoons kosher salt

2 tablespoons sugar

PORK CHOPS

4 bone-in pork chops, 1 to 1¼ inches thick

2 tablespoons sweet BBQ rub

3 tablespoons Lemon Pepper Herb Rub (page 31)

Olive oil, to rub (if not brining)

PICCATA SAUCE

4 tablespoons unsalted butter, divided

2 cloves garlic, minced

½ cup dry white wine or chicken stock

¼ cup freshly squeezed lemon juice (2 lemons)

¼ cup capers, drained

Zest of 1 lemon

1 tablespoon chopped fresh parsley

Kosher salt and freshly ground black pepper

BRINE THE PORK CHOPS (OPTIONAL): Stir together 4 cups water, the kosher salt, and sugar in a container until dissolved. Submerge the pork chops and let soak for 1 hour in the refrigerator. Remove from the brine and pat thoroughly dry.

PREPARE AND GRILL THE PORK CHOPS: Preheat your grill or smoker to medium-high heat (around 400°F). In a small bowl, mix the sweet BBQ rub and lemon pepper rub. If not brining, lightly rub the chops with olive oil, then season generously on all sides with the rub mixture. If brining, apply the rub mixture directly to the dried chops.

Grill the pork chops for 7 to 9 minutes total, flipping every 30 to 45 seconds for even cooking and char, until the internal temperature reaches 140°F. Remove the chops from the grill, tent with foil, and let them rest. The temperature will rise to a perfect 145°F.

MAKE THE PICCATA SAUCE: While chops rest, place a grill-safe saucepan or skillet on the grill (or on a stovetop over medium heat). Melt 2 tablespoons of the butter. Add the garlic cloves and sauté until fragrant, about 30 seconds. Carefully pour in the white wine (or chicken stock) and lemon juice. Bring to a simmer. Stir the capers and lemon zest. Simmer until the sauce has reduced slightly, 2 to 3 minutes.

Remove from the heat and whisk in the remaining 2 tablespoons butter until emulsified and the sauce is glossy. Stir in the parsley. Season to taste with salt and pepper, if needed.

SERVE: Spoon the buttery, tangy piccata sauce generously over the grilled pork chops. Garnish with lemon slices and/or fresh parsley if desired.

FLAVOR BOOST: As soon as the chops come off the grill, hit 'em with a lemon pepper butter bomb. Mash room-temperature butter with lemon zest, black pepper, and a little garlic powder, then let it melt all over while the chops rest and this is a mollywhopper!

BBQ Cubano Sandwich

This ain't your average Cubano. We're flipping the script with smoky pulled pork, grilled deli ham, melty Swiss, crisp pickles, and a BBQ aioli that hits like Fred Warner. Pressed until golden and gooey, it's crunchy, smoky, tangy, and addictive. West Coast swagger meets Cuban sandwich vibes in every bite.

SERVES: 4
PREP TIME: 10 MINUTES
COOK TIME: 15 MINUTES
TOTAL TIME: 25 MINUTES

PULLED PORK

2 cups leftover pulled pork

2 tablespoons of your favorite BBQ sauce

BBQ AIOLI

⅓ cup mayonnaise

1 tablespoon yellow mustard

1 tablespoon of your favorite BBQ sauce

½ teaspoon garlic powder

½ teaspoon smoked paprika

Pinch of salt

SANDWICH BUILD

4 Cuban rolls, hoagie rolls, or sliced sourdough for a West Coast twist

2 tablespoons yellow mustard

16 slices deli ham

8 slices Swiss cheese

12 to 16 dill pickle slices (thinly sliced lengthwise if using whole pickles)

2 tablespoons unsalted butter

REHEAT THE PORK: In a skillet over medium heat, warm the pulled pork with the BBQ sauce to add moisture and flavor. Heat until hot and juicy, stirring occasionally. Set aside.

MAKE THE BBQ AIOLI: In a small bowl, mix together the mayonnaise, yellow mustard, BBQ sauce, garlic powder, smoked paprika, and a pinch of salt until smooth. Set aside.

BUILD THE SANDWICHES: Slice your rolls in half lengthwise. Spread a thin layer of yellow mustard on the inside of the bottom half of each roll. Spread a layer of BBQ aioli on the inside of the top half of each roll.

Layer the sandwiches in the following order on the bottom bun: ½ cup warmed pulled pork, 4 slices deli ham, 2 slices Swiss cheese, ending with 3 to 4 dill pickle slices. Place the top roll on.

GRILL IT: Lightly butter the outsides (top and bottom) of each assembled sandwich. Heat a cast-iron skillet, griddle, or panini press to medium heat. Place the sandwiches on the hot surface. If not using a panini press, press the sandwiches down firmly with a heavy pan, a grill press, or a foil-wrapped brick. Grill for 3 to 4 minutes per side, or until the bread is golden brown and crispy and the cheese is melted and gooey.

BOSS MOVE

Brush the bread with melted butter mixed with a little BBQ sauce before pressing. It crisps up perfect and is the type of move that'll have folks thinking you're running a sandwich shop out back.

The Emperor's Porchetta

A porchetta like no other. I cooked this one up with my chef homie Nate, and the garnishes were his idea. They blew my mind and had everybody at the event talking. Crispy skin, miso, lemongrass, five-spice . . . it's fusion, flavor-packed, and built for backyard legends.

SERVES: 6 TO 8
PREP TIME: 25 MINUTES
CHILL TIME (PORK): OVERNIGHT (TO DRY SKIN)
COOK TIME: 3 TO 4 HOURS
REST TIME: 15 MINUTES

QUICK PICKLED ONION

½ cup rice vinegar

1 tablespoon sugar

½ teaspoon kosher salt

1 small red onion, thinly sliced

PORK

One 4-to-5-pound skin-on pork belly, butterflied for rolling, meat-side scored

2 tablespoons kosher salt, divided

1 tablespoon freshly ground black pepper

FILLING PASTE

2 tablespoons white miso paste

1 tablespoon soy sauce

1 tablespoon fish sauce

1 tablespoon honey

2 tablespoons neutral oil (such as grapeseed or canola)

1 tablespoon Chinese five-spice powder

1 tablespoon lemongrass paste or 1 fresh stalk, white and light green parts only, finely minced

1 tablespoon grated fresh ginger

6 cloves garlic, minced

2 green onions, white parts only, finely chopped

Zest of 1 lime

1 small bunch cilantro, stems and leaves, finely chopped

MANDARIN GARNISH

2 seedless mandarin oranges, peeled and segmented or one small can mandarin oranges, drained

Zest of 1 mandarin (optional, for extra punch)

Small fresh cilantro sprigs, for serving

PICKLE THE ONIONS: In a small bowl, combine the rice vinegar, sugar, and salt. Stir until the sugar and salt dissolve. Add the red onion. Ensure that the onion slices are submerged. Let sit at room temperature for at least 30 minutes, or longer. Can be refrigerated for up to 3 days.

PREP THE PORK: Lay the butterflied pork belly skin-side down. If the meat side isn't already scored, score it in a 1-inch crosshatch pattern, being careful not to cut through to the skin. Season the meat side evenly with 1 tablespoon of the salt and the pepper.

MAKE THE FILLING PASTE: In a bowl, mix all the filling paste ingredients until a smooth paste forms. Spread this paste evenly over the scored-meat side of the pork belly, working it into the scores. Do not apply to the skin.

ROLL AND TIE: Starting from one of the shorter sides, roll the pork belly up tightly into a log. Secure the roll with butcher's twine, tying it every 1 to 2 inches so it maintains its shape during cooking. Pat the skin of the porchetta very dry with paper towels. Rub the remaining 1 tablespoon of salt all over the skin.

Place the rolled porchetta on a wire rack set over a baking sheet. Chill in the refrigerator, uncovered, overnight, or at least 8 hours, to allow the skin to dry out completely. This is key for crispy skin.

ROAST: Preheat your oven or smoker to 300°F. Place the porchetta (still on the wire rack over the tray to catch drippings) into the preheated oven or smoker. Roast for 2½ to 3 hours, or until the internal temperature reaches 160°F.

CRISP THE SKIN: Once the internal temperature is 160°F, increase the oven or smoker heat to 450°F (or use a broiler, watching very carefully). Continue to cook for another 20 to 30 minutes, rotating the porchetta every 10 minutes if needed for even crisping, until the skin is deeply golden brown, blistered, and very crispy (crackling). Keep a close eye on it to prevent burning.

REST AND GARNISH: Remove the porchetta from the oven or smoker and let it rest for at least 15 minutes before slicing. Remove the butcher's twine and slice the porchetta into thick rounds ¾ to 1 inch thick.

SERVE: Arrange slices on a platter or individual plates. Top each slice (or the platter) with a few mandarin orange segments, a small pile of the pickled onions, a touch of mandarin zest, if using, and fresh cilantro sprigs.

BOSS MOVE

After you roll that porchetta, blast the skin with a hair dryer on the cool setting before it chills overnight. It dries it out quick and sets you up for that glass-shattering crackle.

CHAPTER 4

SEAFOOD

THE WHARF WAGON

Welcome to the Wharf Wagon, where surf meets smoke and every bite tastes like a seaside celebration. Every bite in this section is a blessing from The Bay. Buckle up because things are going to get wild, briny, buttery, and bold. We're talkin' smoky shrimp, flame-kissed lobster tails, grilled octopus, crispy-fried fish, and sauces so good you'll be sippin' 'em like chowder. Whether it swam, crawled, or had tentacles, we're giving it the Flavor Train treatment: high heat, big flavor, and no fear. Expect coastal classics with swagger and seafood dishes that'll leave a splash like a cannonball off the pier. Let's dock this thing and dive in.

Flavor You Can Savor

Chuck's Cioppino

Welcome to The Bay Area. This right here is West Coast seafood stew royalty. Loaded with shrimp, clams, mussels, fish, crab, and scallops swimming in a rich, spicy tomato-wine broth laced with chorizo, fennel and fresh herbs. This one will have you feeling like you're sitting in downtown SF while in the comfort of your home.

SERVES: 4 TO 6
PREP TIME: 20 MINUTES
COOK TIME: 45 MINUTES

BASE

2 tablespoons extra-virgin olive oil

6 ounces Basque or Spanish chorizo (not Mexican chorizo), casing removed, diced

1 medium yellow onion, diced

1 small fennel bulb, cored and diced (fronds reserved for garnish, optional)

Kosher salt

4 cloves garlic, minced

1½ teaspoons red pepper flakes, or as needed

1 teaspoon smoked paprika

1 teaspoon dried oregano

½ teaspoon fennel seed, lightly crushed (optional, but nice)

¼ cup tomato paste

1 cup dry white wine (such as Sauvignon Blanc or Pinot Grigio)

Two 14-ounce cans crushed tomatoes (or one 28-ounce can)

4 cups seafood stock (or a mix of clam juice and fish stock or vegetable broth)

Zest of 1 lemon

Freshly ground black pepper

SEAFOOD

½ pound mussels, cleaned and debearded

½ pound clams (littleneck or Manila), scrubbed

½ pound large shrimp (16 to 20 count), peeled and deveined

½ pound firm white fish (halibut, cod, or snapper), cut into 1-inch chunks

½ pound sea scallops (optional)

½ pound squid rings and tentacles (optional)

1 pound cooked Dungeness crab

FOR FINISHING

Juice of ½ lemon, plus more as needed

2 tablespoons unsalted butter, diced

¼ cup chopped fresh parsley

2 tablespoons chopped fresh basil or chives (optional)

FOR SERVING

Grilled sourdough or crusty bread, rubbed with garlic

RENDER THE CHORIZO AND SAUTÉ THE AROMATICS: Heat the olive oil in a large Dutch oven or heavy-bottomed pot over medium heat. Add the chorizo and cook for 4 to 5 minutes, stirring occasionally, until browned, fragrant, and some fat has rendered. Add the onion and fennel bulb to the pot, along with a big pinch of salt. Sauté for 5 to 6 minutes, until softened and translucent.

Stir in the garlic cloves, red pepper flakes, smoked paprika, dried oregano, and ½ teaspoon crushed fennel seed, if using. Cook for 1 minute until fragrant.

BUILD THE SAUCE: Stir in the tomato paste and cook for 2 minutes, stirring constantly, until the mixture darkens slightly in color. Pour in the wine and scrape up any browned bits from the bottom of the pot; this is called deglazing. Let the wine simmer and reduce for 2 to 3 minutes.

LAYER THE BROTH: Add the crushed tomatoes, 4 cups seafood stock, and the lemon zest. Bring the mixture to a simmer. Reduce the heat to medium-low and let it cook uncovered for 15 to 20 minutes to allow the flavors to meld and deepen. Season to taste with salt and black pepper.

ADD THE SEAFOOD IN ORDER: Increase the heat to medium. Add the mussels and clams to the pot. Cover and cook for about 5 minutes, or until most of them have started to open. Gently stir in the shrimp, white fish chunks, sea scallops, if using, and squid, if using. Lastly, add the Dungeness crab. Cover the pot again and simmer for 4 to 5 minutes more, or until the fish is cooked through, the shrimp are pink, and all the shellfish have opened. Discard any mussels or clams that remain closed.

FINISH: Gently stir in the lemon juice, butter, allowing it to melt into the broth, parsley, and basil or chives, if using. Taste the broth one last time and adjust the seasoning (salt, pepper, or lemon juice), if needed.

SERVE HOT: Ladle the cioppino generously into large, shallow bowls. Serve immediately with plenty of grilled sourdough or crusty bread on the side for soaking up the delicious broth. Garnish with the reserved fennel fronds, if desired.

FLAVOR BOOST: Grill some sourdough, rub it with garlic, drizzle olive oil, and hit it with flaky salt—it'll soak up that broth like it owes you money. Wanna go harder? Drop a scoop of garlic herb butter in the bowl. Game. Changer.

Scallops and Risotto

Scallops, a.k.a. sea marshmallows, really are the candy of the sea. Buttery, rich, and crazy good when you nail 'em. Elegant enough for date night, easy enough for a Tuesday, and once you lock in this recipe, you'll never wanna order scallops out again. Make it for someone special and you might just get lucky.

SERVES: 4
PREP TIME: 15 MINUTES
COOK TIME: ABOUT 30 MINUTES (RISOTTO) PLUS 5 MINUTES (SCALLOPS)
TOTAL TIME: 45 MINUTES

SCALLOPS

12 large sea scallops (dry-packed recommended)

Kosher salt and freshly ground black pepper

1 tablespoon extra-virgin olive oil

1 tablespoon unsalted butter

PARMESAN RISOTTO

1 tablespoon extra-virgin olive oil

2 tablespoons unsalted butter

1 small shallot, finely diced

1½ cups Arborio rice

½ cup dry white wine (such as Pinot Grigio or Sauvignon Blanc)

5 cups low-sodium chicken stock, warmed

¾ cup freshly grated Parmesan cheese

Kosher salt and freshly ground black pepper

Chopped fresh parsley or lemon zest, for garnish (optional)

PREPARE THE SCALLOPS: If present, remove the small, tough side muscle from each scallop. Pat the scallops very dry with paper towels. Moisture is the enemy of a good sear. Season both sides of the scallops lightly with salt and pepper. Let them sit at room temperature while you prepare the risotto.

MAKE THE RISOTTO: In a wide saucepan or large, heavy-bottomed skillet, heat the olive oil and butter over medium heat. Add the shallot and cook for 2 to 3 minutes until softened and translucent but not browned. Stir in the rice and cook for 1 to 2 minutes, stirring constantly, to toast the grains until the edges are slightly translucent. Pour in the wine and stir continuously until it is fully absorbed.

Begin adding the warmed stock, one ladleful (about ½ cup) at a time, stirring frequently. Allow each addition of stock to be mostly absorbed before adding the next. Continue this process until the rice is al dente (tender with a slight bite in the center) and the risotto is creamy. This should take 20 to 25 minutes. Once the rice is cooked, remove the risotto from the heat. Stir in the Parmesan cheese. Taste and season with salt and pepper as needed. Keep warm while you cook the scallops.

SEAR THE SCALLOPS: Heat a large stainless steel or cast-iron skillet over medium-high heat until very hot.

Add the olive oil and butter to the hot skillet. Once the butter is melted and foaming, carefully place the seasoned scallops in the pan in a single layer, ensuring they are spaced out and not crowded.

Sear the scallops without moving them for 1½ to 2 minutes on the first side, until a golden-brown crust forms. Flip the scallops and cook for another 1 to 1½ minutes on the other side, until they are just opaque in the center and cooked through. Do not overcook, as they can become rubbery.

SERVE: Spoon a generous portion of the creamy Parmesan risotto into shallow bowls or onto plates. Top each serving with three seared scallops. Garnish with parsley or a little lemon zest, if desired. Serve immediately.

BOSS MOVE

Right after you sear 'em, splash the pan with white wine and hit it with a squeeze of lemon juice. It grabs all those crispy bits and turns into a quick pan sauce that leaves the scallops citrusy, glossy, and bossy.

Stir-Fried Shrimp

I love me some stir-fried noodles, so this one hits home. The secret to that restaurant-level meat? Velveting. You can use spaghetti, but real Shanghai or chow mein noodles take it up a notch. Skip the weak takeout and make this at home instead.

SERVES: 4

PREP TIME: 20 MINUTES (INCLUDES VELVETING REST)

COOK TIME: 10 MINUTES

TOTAL TIME: 30 MINUTES

SHRIMP VELVETING

½ pound shrimp (21 to 25 count), peeled and deveined

½ teaspoon baking soda

STIR-FRY

½ pound Shanghai-style chow mein noodles (see Noodle Options in side bar)

2 tablespoons neutral oil (vegetable or canola), plus 1 teaspoon, divided

2 cloves garlic, minced

½ small yellow onion, thinly sliced

2 scallions, sliced into 2-inch pieces, plus more for garnish

Sesame oil for garnish (optional)

SAUCE

2 tablespoons soy sauce

1 tablespoon oyster sauce

1 tablespoon Shaoxing wine or dry sherry

1 teaspoon sesame oil

1 teaspoon sugar

¼ teaspoon ground white pepper

VELVET THE SHRIMP: In a bowl, toss together the shrimp and baking soda. Let sit for 15 minutes. Rinse the shrimp thoroughly under cold running water to remove all the baking soda. Pat very dry with paper towels.

PREPARE THE NOODLES: Bring a pot of water to a boil. Cook the noodles according to the package directions, until just al dente (typically 2 to 3 minutes for fresh noodles). Drain the noodles, rinse with cold water to stop the cooking process, and toss with 1 teaspoon of neutral oil to prevent sticking. Set aside.

MAKE THE SAUCE: In a small bowl, whisk together the soy sauce, oyster sauce, Shaoxing wine, sesame oil, sugar, and white pepper. Set aside.

STIR-FRY: Heat 1 tablespoon of neutral oil in a wok or large, heavy-bottomed skillet over medium-high heat until shimmering. Add the garlic cloves and yellow onion. Stir-fry for about 30 seconds until fragrant. Remove the shrimp and set aside. Add the remaining 1 tablespoon oil if the wok seems dry.

COMBINE AND FINISH: Add the cooked noodles and scallions to the wok. If you cooked the shrimp separately, add them back now. Pour the prepared sauce over everything. Toss quickly and stir-fry for 2 to 3 minutes, until the noodles and shrimp are hot and coated well with the sauce.

SERVE: Plate immediately. Garnish with scallions or a few drops of sesame oil, if desired.

BOSS MOVE

After you toss it all together, let the noodles sit in the hot wok for about a minute without touching 'em. That's how you build that crispy golden crust on the bottom and that classic chow mein texture.

Noodle Options (authentic Shanghai-style)

Fresh Shanghai noodles: Found in most Asian markets, usually labeled "Shanghai-style noodles" or "thick chow mein noodles." Typically yellow, chewy, and eggless.

Wheat-based knife-cut noodles (Dao Xiao Mian): Thicker and more rustic with chewy edges—these are common in homestyle Shanghai cooking.

Dried lo mein noodles or Hong Kong-style egg noodles: Can work in a pinch, but fresh noodles deliver the best texture. Cook according to the package directions.

Grilled Octopus with Herb Butter

Octopus looks wild, but trust me, it's stupid easy. Too nervous? Grab it pre-cooked and call it a day. Toss those tentacles on a hot grill till they're crispy outside, tender inside, then drench 'em in lemon-herb butter that melts into every groove. Restaurant-level flavor you can flex right at home, no stress.

SERVES: 4

PREP TIME: 15 MINUTES

COOK TIME: 10 TO 12 MINUTES (GRILL OR SEAR FOR RAW) OR 5 TO 6 MINUTES (GRILL OR SEAR FOR PRE-COOKED)

NOTE: ADD 1½ TO 2 HOURS SIMMERING TIME IF USING RAW TENTACLES

OCTOPUS TENTACLES (CHOOSE YOUR TYPE)

RAW TENTACLES

Kosher salt

1 lemon, halved

1 onion, quartered

4 cloves garlic, smashed

2 bay leaves

1 teaspoon freshly cracked black peppercorns

2 to 2½ pounds raw octopus tentacles, cleaned and separated

PRE-COOKED TENTACLES

2 to 2½ pounds pre-cooked octopus tentacles (vacuum-packed or frozen)

1 tablespoon extra-virgin olive oil (optional)

Squeeze of fresh lemon juice (optional)

1 clove garlic, minced (optional)

COMPOUND HERB BUTTER

½ cup unsalted butter, at room temperature

1 tablespoon finely chopped fresh parsley

1 tablespoon finely chopped fresh chives

1 teaspoon finely chopped fresh tarragon or dill

2 cloves garlic, grated

Zest of 1 lemon (save the lemon for finishing; optional)

1 teaspoon Dijon mustard

Pinch of flaky salt

Freshly ground black pepper

PREPARE THE OCTOPUS (IF USING RAW TENTACLES): Bring a large pot of water to a simmer. Add a generous pinch of kosher salt, the halved lemon, quartered onion, smashed garlic cloves, bay leaves, and peppercorns. Add the raw tentacles and simmer gently for 1½ to 2 hours, or until tender when pierced with a fork. Drain and allow to cool slightly. Pat thoroughly dry before grilling.

PREPARE THE OCTOPUS (IF USING PRE-COOKED TENTACLES): Thaw the pre-cooked tentacles completely if frozen. Pat thoroughly dry.

Optional: For extra flavor, in a large bowl, toss the pre-cooked tentacles with the olive oil, a squeeze of lemon juice, and a minced garlic clove. Let marinate for 15 to 30 minutes at room temperature.

MAKE THE COMPOUND HERB BUTTER: In a small bowl, combine the butter, parsley, chives, tarragon or dill, grated garlic, lemon zest, Dijon mustard, flaky salt, and pepper to taste. Mix with a fork until thoroughly combined and smooth. Set aside at room temperature (this helps the butter combo melt beautifully over the hot octopus).

GRILL OR SEAR THE OCTOPUS: Preheat your grill to high heat, 450°F to 550°F, or heat a large cast-iron skillet over high heat until smoking hot. Lightly oil the tentacles, if not already marinated.

FOR RAW, SIMMERED TENTACLES: Grill or sear for 2 to 3 minutes per side, until nicely charred and crispy in spots.

FOR PRE-COOKED TENTACLES: Grill or sear for 1 to 2 minutes per side, just to heat through and achieve char marks. *Embrace the char!*

SERVE: Arrange the grilled tentacles on a platter. Immediately spoon or dollop generous amounts of the compound herb butter over the hot tentacles, allowing it to melt down into all the crevices. Finish with an extra squeeze of fresh lemon juice and another sprinkle of flaky salt, if desired. Serve at once.

BOSS MOVE

After grilling, toss the tentacles in a bowl with a spoonful of the compound butter and a splash of sherry vinegar before plating. That sherry vinegar adds that extra chef-y balance that makes people swear you trained in Spain.

Miso Lobster Tails

Lobster's one of my favorite things, and yeah, it's always fire just simply grilled with butter . . . but these tails hit even harder. They're drenched in a ginger-garlic miso butter and it's flavor packin'. I love miso because it brings that umami punch that somehow makes the lobster taste even sweeter. The under-butter trick keeps the meat juicy, and every bite melts like seafood gold.

SERVES: 4
PREP TIME: 10 MINUTES
COOK TIME: 15 MINUTES
TOTAL TIME: 25 MINUTES

LOBSTER TAILS

4 lobster tails, 5 to 6 ounces each

2 tablespoons unsalted butter, at room temperature, for under-the-tail meat

Kosher salt

GINGER-GARLIC MISO BUTTER

½ cup unsalted butter

8 cloves garlic, finely minced

1½ tablespoons grated fresh ginger

1 tablespoon soy sauce

1 tablespoon fish sauce

1 tablespoon white miso paste

PREP THE LOBSTER TAILS: Using sharp kitchen shears, cut lengthwise through the top center of each lobster tail shell, stopping just before the tail fan. Carefully pry the shell halves apart. Gently lift the lobster meat up from the bottom shell, keeping it attached at the base of the tail. Lift the meat and rest it on top of the shell (piggyback style). Spread about ½ tablespoon of butter underneath the lifted lobster meat, directly on the inside of the shell. This helps keep the meat moist.

MAKE THE GINGER-GARLIC MISO BUTTER: In a small saucepan over low heat, melt the butter. Add the garlic cloves and ginger. Cook for 1 to 2 minutes until fragrant, being careful not to brown the garlic. Stir in the soy sauce, fish sauce, and white miso paste. Whisk continuously until the miso paste is fully dissolved and the mixture is emulsified and smooth. Keep warm over very low heat.

GRILL OR SEAR THE LOBSTER TAILS: Preheat your grill or a large cast-iron pan to medium-high heat. Lightly season the exposed lobster meat with salt. Place the lobster tails flesh-side down directly on the hot grill grates or in the preheated pan. Cook for 2 to 3 minutes until lightly charred and grill marks appear. Flip the lobster tails so they are shell-side down.

BASTE AND FINISH: Immediately baste the lobster meat generously with the warm ginger-garlic miso butter. Continue to cook shell-side down, basting occasionally with more miso butter, for another 4 to 5 minutes, or until the lobster meat is opaque and cooked through; the internal temperature should reach 135°F to 140°F.

SERVE: Remove the lobster tails from the heat. Give them a final baste with any remaining miso butter.

Serve hot, with any extra miso butter drizzled on top or served on the side for dipping.

FLAVOR BOOST: Right before the final baste, squeeze a little lime over the lobster and hit it with chili crisp or togarashi. Flavor elevation!

Chuck's Teriyaki Salmon

I've been making this salmon since high school, and now it's one of my wife's and daughter's favorites. Perfect sear, sticky-sweet glaze, and that homemade teriyaki really makes the difference. It's rich, gingery, and salty-sweet in all the right ways. Serve it over rice or noodles if you want, but the fish always steals the show.

SERVES: 4

PREP TIME: 10 MINUTES PLUS COOLING

COOK TIME: 8 TO 10 MINUTES (SALMON) PLUS 10 MINUTES (SAUCE)

REST TIME (SALMON): 5 MINUTES

CHUCK'D UP TERIYAKI SAUCE

½ cup soy sauce

¼ cup packed dark brown sugar

2 tablespoons honey

2 tablespoons rice vinegar

1 tablespoon sesame oil

2 cloves garlic, finely grated or minced

1 tablespoon grated fresh ginger

1 tablespoon mirin (optional, enhances flavor)

1 teaspoon cornstarch mixed with 1 tablespoon cold water

SALMON

4 salmon fillets, 6 ounces each, skin-on preferred

1 tablespoon neutral oil (such as avocado or canola), plus more for coating the fish (optional)

Kosher salt and freshly ground black pepper

GARNISH

Toasted sesame seeds

Thinly sliced scallions

Chili crisp or red pepper flakes (optional, for a kick)

Lime wedges

BUILD THE TERIYAKI SAUCE: In a small saucepan, combine the soy sauce, dark brown sugar, honey, rice vinegar, sesame oil, garlic cloves, ginger, and mirin, if using. Bring the mixture to a simmer over medium heat, stirring occasionally, for 3 to 4 minutes to dissolve the sugar and meld the flavors.

Stir the cornstarch slurry into the simmering sauce. Continue to simmer, stirring constantly, until the sauce thickens slightly—enough to coat the back of a spoon, 1 to 2 minutes. Remove from the heat and let the mixture cool slightly while you prepare the salmon. The sauce will thicken more as it cools.

PREP THE SALMON: Pat the salmon fillets very dry with paper towels. This is crucial for crispy skin. Lightly rub the fillets with a very thin layer of oil (or you can add the oil directly to the pan). Season both sides with salt and pepper.

SEAR LIKE A PRO: Heat the neutral oil in a large nonstick or cast-iron skillet over medium-high heat until the oil is shimmering and just shy of smoking. Gently place the salmon fillets skin-side down in the hot skillet. Sear undisturbed for 3 to 4 minutes, or until the skin is very crispy and golden brown and easily releases from the pan. Carefully flip the salmon fillets. Cook on the flesh side for another 2 to 3 minutes. In the last minute of cooking, brush or spoon some of the prepared teriyaki sauce over the salmon. Cook until the internal temperature reaches 125°F to 130°F for medium. Be careful not to overcook; salmon cooks quickly.

LET IT REST: Remove the salmon from the skillet and place it on a clean plate. Tent loosely with foil and let it rest for 5 minutes. This allows the juices to redistribute, keeping the salmon tender and luscious.

FINISH AND SERVE: Brush the rested salmon with more teriyaki sauce or spoon it over generously. Garnish with toasted sesame seeds, thinly sliced scallions, and chili crisp or red pepper flakes (if using).

Serve with lime wedges on the side for squeezing. Plate it over garlic butter rice, soba noodles, or even a tangy Asian slaw.

BOSS MOVE

After the sear, splash the hot pan with lime juice and a little extra teriyaki to make a quick glaze bomb. Spoon it over the salmon while it rests, then finish with chili crisp for a delicious sweet-heat-umami combo!

Crispy Fishwich

I never liked fish sandwiches. Then I realized it's just 'cause most spots don't make 'em right. This one does: golden, crunchy beer-battered fish stacked on a toasted brioche bun with lemon-sriracha slaw and garlicky aioli. Crispy, tangy, creamy, bold . . . it shuts down any sandwich competition. Grab it with both hands and let the crumbs fall where they may.

SERVES: 4
PREP TIME: 20 MINUTES (INCLUDES SAUCE AND SLAW PREP)
COOK TIME: 15 TO 20 MINUTES
TOTAL TIME: 40 MINUTES

GARLIC AIOLI

- ½ cup mayonnaise
- 1 clove garlic, finely minced or grated
- 1 tablespoon freshly squeezed lemon juice
- 1 teaspoon Dijon mustard
- Kosher salt and freshly ground black pepper

LEMON-SRIRACHA SLAW

- ¼ cup mayonnaise
- 1½ tablespoons freshly squeezed lemon juice
- 1½ teaspoons lemon zest
- 1 tablespoon sriracha, or as needed
- ½ tablespoon honey
- 3 cups shredded green cabbage or packaged coleslaw mix
- Kosher salt and freshly ground black pepper

FISH

- Vegetable oil or canola oil, for frying
- 1 to 1½ pounds firm white fish fillets (cod, haddock, or halibut), cut into 4 sandwich-size pieces
- Kosher salt and freshly ground black pepper
- One 5-ounce package McCormick Golden Dipt Beer Batter Mix
- ¾ cup cold beer (Miller Lite or similar light lager recommended)
- 1 teaspoon hot sauce (optional, for a kick in the batter)

FOR ASSEMBLY

- 4 soft sandwich buns or brioche rolls
- Unsalted butter or oil, for toasting the buns
- Dill pickle slices (optional)
- Extra lemon wedges, for serving

MAKE THE GARLIC AIOLI: In a small bowl, whisk together the mayonnaise, garlic clove, lemon juice, and Dijon mustard. Season with salt and pepper to taste. Cover and chill in the refrigerator for 10 minutes to let the flavors meld.

MAKE THE LEMON-SRIRACHA SLAW: In a mixing bowl, whisk together the mayonnaise, lemon juice, lemon zest, sriracha, and honey. Add the shredded cabbage and toss until evenly coated. Season to taste with salt and pepper. Cover and refrigerate while you prepare the fish.

HEAT THE OIL AND PREP THE FISH: In a deep skillet, Dutch oven, or deep fryer over medium-high heat, heat 1½ to 2 inches of oil to 350°F to 365°F. Use a thermometer to monitor the temperature. While the oil heats, pat the fish fillets dry with paper towels and season lightly with salt and pepper.

In a medium bowl, whisk together the batter mix, beer, and hot sauce, if using, until smooth. Let the batter rest for 5 minutes.

FRY THE FISH: Once the oil is hot, dip the seasoned fish in the beer batter, letting the excess drip off. Fry in batches for 4 to 6 minutes, turning once, until golden, crisp, and cooked through. The crust will be a deep golden color, the fish will appear firm, flake easily and temp around 145 degrees internal.

Remove the fish with a slotted spoon and drain on a rack over paper towels. Season with salt.

TOAST THE BUNS: While the fish rests for a moment, butter or oil the buns and toast cut-side down until golden.

ASSEMBLE THE SANDWICH: Spread garlic aioli on both sides, add a fried fish fillet, top with lemon-sriracha slaw and pickles, and serve with lemon wedges.

LEVEL UP: Keep the batter cold and the oil hot for a crisp crust. Don't overcrowd the fryer—too much fish cools the oil and makes it soggy.

A splash of malt vinegar or squeeze of lemon juice adds a classic tang before closing the sandwich.

BOSS MOVE

Right before stacking, hit that hot fish with a splash of malt vinegar and a squeeze of lemon. Wanna get wicked? Slide a slice of sharp cheddar under the fish and torch it till it's bubbling.

Easy Street Shrimp

Stupid easy. Ridiculously tasty. These shrimp hit the smoker and drink up flavor like they've been stranded in the desert. Twenty minutes later, you've got buttery, smoky shrimp that taste like five-star magic for back-yard effort. Just don't forget the grilled bread to soak up every last drop.

SERVES: 4 AS AN APPETIZER OR LIGHT MEAL
PREP TIME: 10 MINUTES
MARINATE TIME: 20 MINUTES
SMOKE TIME: 20 MINUTES
TOTAL TIME: 50 MINUTES

SHRIMP

1 pound large raw shrimp (16 to 20 count), peeled and deveined (tail-on optional)

1 tablespoon extra-virgin olive oil

1 tablespoon soy sauce

1½ tablespoons Cajun seasoning (use your favorite store-bought or make your own)

BUTTER BATH

½ cup unsalted butter

6 cloves garlic, finely minced

Zest of 1 lemon (about ½ tablespoon)

1 tablespoon freshly squeezed lemon juice

3 to 4 small fresh rosemary sprigs or 2 large sprigs

GARNISHES (OPTIONAL)

Lemon wedges, for squeezing

Chopped fresh parsley or chives, for color

FOR SERVING

Crusty grilled sourdough bread, for mopping up the butter

MARINATE THE SHRIMP: In a medium bowl, combine the shrimp, olive oil, soy sauce, and Cajun seasoning. Toss well to ensure the shrimp are evenly coated. Let marinate at room temperature for 20 minutes while you prepare the butter bath and preheat the smoker.

PREP THE BUTTER BATH: In a small saucepan over low heat, melt the butter. Stir in the garlic, lemon zest, and lemon juice. Let the mixture gently infuse over very low heat for 2 to 3 minutes, stirring occasionally. Be careful not to let the garlic brown or burn. Remove from the heat.

ARRANGE THE SHRIMP FOR SMOKING: Lay the marinated shrimp in a single layer in a small, smoker-safe foil pan or a small cast-iron skillet. Pour the prepared lemon-garlic butter evenly over the shrimp. Tuck the rosemary sprigs around and over the shrimp to infuse maximum aroma during smoking.

SMOKE THE SHRIMP: Preheat your smoker to 300°F. Place the pan containing the shrimp and butter bath directly on the smoker grates. Smoke for approximately 20 minutes, or until the shrimp are pink, firm, and just cooked through. Shrimp cook quickly, so be careful not to overcook them.

SERVE: Carefully remove the pan from the smoker. Serve immediately. Garnish with lemon wedges for squeezing, and parsley or chives, if desired. Don't forget crusty grilled sourdough bread to mop up every last drop of that delicious butter.

BOSS MOVE

Throw a splash of hot sauce and a shot of bourbon into the butter bath before it hits the smoker. It cranks the heat, deepens the flavor, and turns that sauce into smoky, spicy velvet that'll have people fighting for the last hunk of bread.

Marinated Dungeness Crab

Growing up in the Bay, Dungeness crab is like religion, and this right here feels like a holy experience. Most people don't marinate their crab, but once you do, it's like unlocking a whole new flavor dimension. Easy to prep ahead and loaded with punchy freshness that you're gonna love. This is the kind of dish that makes people stop talking and just start cracking shells.

SERVES: 4 AS AN APPETIZER
PREP TIME: 15 MINUTES (IF CRAB IS PRE-CLEANED)
MARINATE TIME: AT LEAST 4 HOURS, UP TO OVERNIGHT
COOK TIME: 0 (CRAB IS PRE-COOKED)

2 whole cooked Dungeness crabs (2 to 2½ pounds each), cleaned and sectioned

¼ cup extra-virgin olive oil

3 tablespoons rice vinegar or white wine vinegar

2 tablespoons soy sauce

¼ to ⅓ cup freshly squeezed lemon juice (2 lemons)

Zest of 1 lemon

6 cloves garlic, smashed or coarsely chopped

½ teaspoon red pepper flakes (or more, if you like heat)

1 tablespoon chopped fresh parsley or cilantro

Kosher salt and freshly ground black pepper

Splash of Roscato wine or other sweet white or rosé wine (optional)

Crab crackers and crusty bread, for serving

PREPARE YOUR CRAB: If your cooked Dungeness crabs are not already cleaned and sectioned: Remove the top shell (carapace), gills (feathery parts), and the apron (tail flap on the underside). Rinse the body cavity. Break or cut the crab body into sections (usually quarters or halves). Separate the legs and claws.

Lightly crack the claws and larger leg segments with the back of a heavy knife or a crab cracker to allow the marinade to penetrate better. Be gentle to keep the meat intact.

MIX THE MARINADE: In a large, non-reactive bowl (glass or stainless steel), combine the olive oil, vinegar, soy sauce, lemon juice to taste, the lemon zest, garlic cloves, red pepper flakes, and parsley or cilantro. Whisk well. Add a good pinch of kosher salt and black pepper. Taste and adjust the seasoning if necessary. If using, add the wine here.

MARINATE THE CRAB: Add the prepared crab pieces to the marinade. Toss gently but thoroughly to ensure all crab pieces are well coated with the marinade. Transfer the crab and all the marinade to a large zip-top bag or a covered container. Refrigerate for at least 4 hours, preferably overnight, to allow the flavors to fully infuse. You can gently turn the bag or stir the crab occasionally to redistribute the marinade.

SERVE: Remove the marinated crab from the refrigerator 10 to 15 minutes before serving to let it come slightly to room temperature; this enhances the flavor. Arrange the crab pieces on a platter or in a large bowl, drizzling any remaining marinade over the top. Serve chilled, with plenty of napkins, crab crackers, and small forks or picks. Crusty bread is excellent for soaking up the marinade.

BOSS MOVE

Before serving, toss the crab with a few spoonfuls of warm garlic butter mixed with a splash of the leftover marinade. It wakes everything up and adds a rich, silky coating that clings to every bite. Serve with warm sourdough to soak up that magic. It's the ultimate mop-up moment.

Aguachile Verde Fresco

Growing up in Cali, this dish was everywhere thanks to the Mexican influence, and for good reason. Cold, spicy, and hella refreshing. These lime-cured shrimp swim in a bold green marinade loaded with chile, garlic, cucumber, and cilantro. And it's crazy easy to whip up! Scoop it with chips, stack it on tostadas, or just crush it by the spoonful. No stove, no sweat, just pure flavor.

SERVES: 4 AS AN APPETIZER
PREP TIME: 15 MINUTES
MARINATE TIME: 20 TO 30 MINUTES
CHILL TIME: 10 TO 15 MINUTES
TOTAL TIME: 45 TO 60 MINUTES

SHRIMP

1 pound raw large shrimp (16 to 20 count), peeled, deveined, and butterflied

½ teaspoon kosher salt

½ cup freshly squeezed lime juice (6 to 8 limes, enough to just cover shrimp)

AGUACHILE MARINADE

½ cup freshly squeezed lime juice, plus more as needed

4 cloves garlic, lightly charred on a dry skillet or grill (optional)

2 serrano chiles, stemmed (to your heat preference)

1 jalapeño, seeded for less heat; leave if you want lots of heat

½ cup, coarsely chopped peeled cucumber

¼ small white onion, coarsely chopped; lightly charred (optional)

1 small bunch cilantro, coarsely chopped (stems included for flavor)

1 teaspoon kosher salt, plus more as needed

1 tablespoon extra-virgin olive oil

2 teaspoons fish sauce (optional, for an umami boost)

TOPPINGS AND FOR SERVING

½ medium red onion, thinly sliced

½ medium cucumber, peeled (or unpeeled), thinly sliced or cut into half-moons

¼ cup fresh cilantro leaves

4 to 6 radishes, thinly sliced (optional)

1 fresh chile (serrano or jalapeño), thinly sliced (optional, for heat)

Tortilla chips or tostadas

PREP AND "COOK" THE SHRIMP: Place the butterflied shrimp in a shallow, non-reactive dish (glass or ceramic). Season with salt and pour the lime juice over them, ensuring they are just covered by the juice. Gently toss to coat. Cover and refrigerate for 20 to 30 minutes, or until the shrimp turn opaque and appear "cooked" by the citrus acid.

MAKE THE *AGUACHILE* MARINADE: While the shrimp marinate in a blender, combine the lime juice, garlic cloves, if using, serrano chiles, jalapeño, cucumber, white onion, if using, cilantro, salt, olive oil, and fish sauce, if using. Blend until the marinade is smooth and bright green. Taste and adjust for salt, lime juice, and heat (for more, add more chile) to your liking.

COMBINE AND CHILL: Once the shrimp are opaque, drain most of the lime juice they were marinating in, leaving only 2 to 3 tablespoons in the dish with the shrimp. Pour the prepared *aguachile verde* marinade over the shrimp. Gently toss to combine. Return the shrimp to the refrigerator to chill for 10 to 15 minutes more, allowing the flavors to meld and the shrimp to absorb the green marinade.

ASSEMBLE AND SERVE: On a chilled serving platter or in a shallow bowl, arrange a layer of red onion and sliced cucumber. Spoon the marinated shrimp and the *aguachile verde* sauce over the bed of onion and cucumber. Garnish generously with cilantro, thinly sliced radishes, if using, and sliced chile (for presentation and heat, if you like). Serve immediately while cold, with tortilla chips or tostadas on the side for scooping.

LEVEL UP: Use fresh lime juice for the brightest flavor—bottled won't compare. Don't over-marinate; once shrimp turn opaque, they're ready. Serve cold and zesty, adjusting chile heat to taste.

BOSS MOVE

Chill your serving dish in the freezer before plating and drizzle a little extra olive oil and flaky salt over the top right before serving. It keeps everything icy cold and adds a silky pop at the finish.

Luxurious Lobster Sando

This is like an East Coast classic crashing the state fair. Beer-battered lobster tail fried golden and stacked on a toasted brioche with crisp lettuce and a creamy, spicy sriracha-Kewpie sauce that sings louder than a stadium crowd. Rich, crispy, buttery, and bougie comfort food you can hold in one hand if your grip game's strong.

SERVES: 2
PREP TIME: 15 MINUTES
COOK TIME: 10 MINUTES
TOTAL TIME: 25 MINUTES

LOBSTER TAILS

1 colossal lobster tail (10 to 12 ounces) or 2 smaller tails (5 to 6 ounces each)

1 cup seasoned seafood breading mix (Louisiana Fish Fry, Zatarain's, or similar)

½ cup cold light beer (Miller Lite, Modelo, or your favorite cold lager)

Vegetable or canola oil, for frying

SRIRACHA-KEWPIE SAUCE

½ cup Kewpie mayonnaise or regular mayonnaise

1 tablespoon sriracha, plus more as needed

1 tablespoon freshly squeezed lemon juice, plus more as needed

SANDWICH

2 brioche buns or split-top rolls

Shredded iceberg or romaine lettuce

Thinly sliced pickles or a small amount of tangy coleslaw (for extra crunch; optional)

PREP THE LOBSTER: If using one colossal tail, use kitchen shears to carefully cut through the top shell lengthwise. Gently remove the lobster meat from the shell in one piece. If the tail has a natural curl, insert a wooden skewer lengthwise through the meat to help keep it straight during frying (optional). If using two smaller tails, prepare them similarly. Pat the lobster meat dry.

MAKE THE SRIRACHA-KEWPIE SAUCE: In a small bowl, whisk together the mayonnaise, sriracha, and lemon juice until well combined. Taste and adjust the heat (more sriracha) or acidity (more lemon juice) to your liking. Chill until ready to use.

BREAD AND FRY THE LOBSTER: In a shallow bowl or dish, combine the breading mix and cold light beer. Whisk until you have a smooth batter, similar in consistency to pancake batter. Let it rest for 2 to 3 minutes.

Heat 1 to 1½ inches oil in a deep pan, Dutch oven, or deep fryer over medium-high heat to 350°F. Ensure you have enough oil for the lobster to float.

Dip each piece of lobster meat (skewered or unskewered) into the beer batter, ensuring it's fully coated and allowing any excess batter to drip off. Carefully lower the battered lobster into the hot oil. Fry for 2 to 3 minutes per side, or until the batter is golden brown, very crispy, and the lobster meat is cooked through; it should be opaque. The exact time will depend on the thickness of the lobster. Remove the fried lobster from the oil and drain on a wire rack set over paper towels. If skewered, carefully remove the skewers.

ASSEMBLE THE SANDWICH: Lightly toast your brioche buns or split-top rolls until golden. Slather both cut sides of the toasted buns generously with the sriracha-Kewpie sauce. Place a layer of shredded lettuce on the bottom bun. Place one fried lobster tail (or half of the colossal tail) on top of the lettuce. Add sliced pickles or a bit of slaw, if using. Place the top bun on and serve immediately while the lobster is hot and crispy.

BOSS MOVE

Before battering, brush your lobster tail with melted butter, garlic, and lemon zest. Let it soak for a minute, then dip in the batter. It locks in big flavor and turns every bite into lobster fireworks under that crispy coat.

Shrimp Not So Po' Boy

This sandwich doesn't just go off, it hits like a brass band rolling through Bourbon Street. Crispy fried buttermilk shrimp piled into a toasted French roll with lettuce, juicy tomato, and pickles, all drowned in a tangy caper remoulade that hits every note. The flavors are so luxurious it's a po'boy only in name because this sandwich is money!

SERVES: 4
PREP TIME: 15 MINUTES
MARINATE TIME: 20 TO 30 MINUTES
CHILL TIME: 10 MINUTES
COOK TIME: 15 MINUTES
TOTAL TIME: 50 TO 60 MINUTES

SHRIMP

$1\frac{1}{2}$ pounds large shrimp (21 to 25 count), peeled and deveined, tails removed

1 cup buttermilk

2 teaspoons hot sauce (such as Crystal or Tabasco)

DREDGE

1 cup all-purpose flour

½ cup fine cornmeal

1 tablespoon of your favorite Cajun rub or seasoning

CAPER REMOULADE

½ cup mayonnaise

1 tablespoon Dijon mustard or Creole mustard

1 tablespoon ketchup

1 tablespoon dill pickle juice or caper juice

2 teaspoons prepared horseradish

1 small clove garlic, finely grated or minced

1 teaspoon hot sauce, plus more as needed

½ teaspoon paprika (smoked or sweet)

1 tablespoon capers, finely chopped

½ teaspoon caper brine (optional, for extra tang)

Pinch of cayenne pepper (optional)

Kosher salt and freshly ground black pepper

FOR FRYING

Neutral oil (peanut or canola recommended)

Kosher salt

FOR SERVING

4 French rolls or hoagie buns (sturdy, but soft inside)

2 cups shredded iceberg lettuce

2 medium ripe tomatoes, thinly sliced

1 cup dill pickle chips or slices

Hot sauce (optional)

MARINATE THE SHRIMP: In a large bowl, combine the peeled and deveined shrimp, buttermilk, and hot sauce. Toss to coat, cover, and chill for 20 minutes.

PREPARE THE DREDGE: In a shallow bowl, whisk together the all-purpose flour, cornmeal, and Cajun rub. Set aside.

MAKE THE CAPER REMOULADE: In a small bowl, whisk together the mayo, mustard, ketchup, pickle juice, horseradish, garlic, hot sauce, paprika, capers, and caper brine (optional). Season with cayenne, salt, and pepper. Chill about 10 minutes.

FRY THE SHRIMP: Heat 2 inches of neutral oil to 350°F in a deep skillet or fryer. Remove the shrimp from the marinade, shake off excess marinade, and dredge the shrimp in the flour-cornmeal mix. Fry in batches for 2 to 3 minutes per side until golden and crisp. Transfer to a wire rack and sprinkle lightly with salt.

TOAST THE ROLLS: Split your French rolls lengthwise and toast the cut sides until golden in a skillet, on a griddle, or under a broiler.

ASSEMBLE THE PO' BOYS AND SERVE: Spread remoulade on both sides of each roll. Layer lettuce, tomato, and pickles on the bottom, pile on 6 to 8 shrimp, drizzle with more remoulade or hot sauce, top it off, and serve right away.

LEVEL UP: Serve the po' boys immediately while the shrimp are hot and crispy. They are normally accompanied with French fries, potato chips, or a crisp side slaw.

BOSS MOVE

Right after frying, toss those shrimp in a little garlic butter or a few hits of hot sauce to keep 'em juicy and loaded with flavor. Bonus move: Toast the rolls with a smear of that caper remoulade so every bite comes through with extra heat and tang.

Grilled Bougie Butter Oysters

My wife and I have always been oyster fiends, crushing them by the dozen since we started dating, but these cooked oysters are next-level. They are essentially little flavor grenades from the sea, and because they are cooked, they are the perfect way to get any oyster skeptics on board. For a golden crust, you can sprinkle them with Parmesan, or if you want to get wild, hit them with some hot sauce.

SERVES: 4 AS AN APPETIZER
PREP TIME: 10 MINUTES
COOK TIME: 15 MINUTES
TOTAL TIME: 25 MINUTES

WHITE WINE–GARLIC BUTTER

½ cup unsalted butter

6 cloves garlic, finely minced

1 small shallot, finely minced

½ teaspoon red pepper flakes (optional, for a touch of heat)

⅓ cup dry white wine (such as Sauvignon Blanc or Pinot Grigio)

1 tablespoon freshly squeezed lemon juice

Zest of 1 lemon

1 tablespoon chopped fresh chives

Kosher salt and freshly ground black pepper

OYSTERS

12 fresh oysters, scrubbed clean

¼ cup grated Parmesan or Pecorino Romano cheese (optional, for a savory crust)

Chopped fresh chives, for garnish

Hot sauce or chili crisp, for finishing (optional)

Lemon wedges, for serving

Crusty bread, for serving

MAKE THE WHITE WINE–GARLIC BUTTER: In a small saucepan over medium heat, melt the butter. Add the garlic cloves, shallot, and red pepper flakes, if using. Sauté for 2 to 3 minutes until the garlic and shallot are fragrant and softened but not browned. Carefully pour in the wine. Let it simmer and reduce slightly for about 3 minutes.

Stir in the lemon juice, lemon zest, and chives. Season with salt and black pepper to taste. Remove from the heat and set aside, keeping the mixture warm.

PREPARE YOUR GRILL: Preheat a charcoal or gas grill to medium-high heat (400°F to 450°F). If using charcoal, bank the coals to one side to create an indirect heat zone, if needed, though direct heat is fine for oysters if watched carefully. You can place a cast-iron oyster rack, a flat metal baking sheet, or even crumpled foil directly on the grill grates to create a stable surface for the oysters and to preheat.

SHUCK THE OYSTERS: Carefully shuck the oysters, making sure to preserve as much of their natural brine (liquor) in the deeper half-shell as possible. Use an oyster knife to sever the muscle connecting the oyster meat to the bottom shell so it's loose. Set each shucked oyster (in its deep half-shell) on the preheated rack, baking sheet, or directly on the grill grates, if stable.

GRILL AND BASTE: Spoon about 1 tablespoon of garlic butter over each oyster, then top with cheese if desired. Grill for 5 to 7 minutes, covered or uncovered, until the butter bubbles and the oyster edges curl.

SERVE HOT: Using tongs, remove the hot oysters to a platter. Garnish with hot sauce, and serve immediately with lemon wedges and crusty bread.

FLAVOR BOOST: Stir Calabrian chili paste into the garlic butter before grilling. It adds smoky depth and a slow-burn heat that turns every flavor grenade into a flavor bomb!

Shrimp Scampi 2.0

Ya'll remember* Pimp My Ride? *Well this is* Pimp My Shrimp, *a simple but succulent spin on the classic scampi that's bold, buttery, and loaded with flavor. Juicy shrimp swimming in garlic-butter sauce with that tangy pop that hits like a DJ drop. It's the kind of dish that'll impress your Nonna and have your homies fighting for the last bite.

SERVES: 4
PREP TIME: 25 MINUTES
COOK TIME: 15 MINUTES

SHRIMP

1 pound large shrimp, peeled and deveined

1 cup buttermilk or 1 cup milk plus 1 tablespoon freshly squeezed lemon juice

1 cup all-purpose flour

1 cup fine Italian breadcrumbs

1 cup cornstarch

1 teaspoon garlic powder

1 teaspoon dried oregano

1 teaspoon red pepper flakes

Kosher salt and freshly ground black pepper

Vegetable oil, for frying

BUTTER SAUCE

6 tablespoons unsalted butter

6 cloves garlic, minced

1 cup dry white wine (such as Pinot Grigio or Sauvignon Blanc)

Zest and juice of 1 lemon

2 tablespoons finely chopped fresh parsley

1 tablespoon finely chopped fresh basil (optional, but do it)

Kosher salt and freshly ground black pepper

2 tablespoons grated Parmigiano-Reggiano cheese

MARINATE THE SHRIMP: In a medium bowl, toss the shrimp in the buttermilk. Let them sit while you prepare the dredge.

DREDGE SETUP: In a bowl, combine the flour, breadcrumbs, cornstarch, garlic powder, oregano, red pepper flakes, and salt and black pepper to taste.

HEAT THE OIL: Heat about 2 inches of vegetable oil in a deep pan over medium-high heat to 350°F.

FRY 'EM UP: Remove the shrimp from the marinade, dredge them in the flour mixture, and fry in the hot oil in batches until golden and crispy (2 to 3 minutes per batch). Drain on a wire rack.

MAKE THE SAUCE: In a skillet, melt the butter over medium heat. Add the minced garlic and cook until fragrant, about 30 seconds. Pour in the white wine and let the mixture reduce slightly, 1 to 2 minutes. Add the lemon zest, lemon juice, parsley, basil, if using, and a pinch of salt and pepper. Finish with the grated cheese and swirl to melt.

TOSS AND SERVE: Gently toss the fried shrimp in the butter sauce or drizzle it over the shrimp right before serving.

BOSS MOVE

Toss the shrimp in butter sauce, hit 'em with lemony parm and flaky salt, then torch the tops for a cheesy, fire-kissed finish.

Grilled Halibut with Spicy Garlic Butter

If you've ever wanted to cook something that looks straight off a restaurant plate but takes zero effort, this is it. Halibut's clean, buttery flavor makes it perfect for anyone who's on the fence about fish. It's not "fishy," it's fancy without trying, and it hits with a spicy lemon garlic butter that'll have you feeling like a pro chef in flip-flops. This one's easy, quick, and packed with flavor that tastes way more complicated than it is. Backyard grill, gourmet vibes, guaranteed applause.

SERVES: 4
PREP TIME: 20 MINUTES (INCLUDES SAUCE AND SLAW PREP)
COOK TIME: 15 TO 20 MINUTES
TOTAL TIME: 40 MINUTES

FISH

- 4 halibut fillets (about 6 ounces each)
- 1 tablespoon olive oil
- 1 teaspoon kosher salt
- ½ teaspoon cracked black pepper
- ½ teaspoon smoked paprika
- ½ teaspoon garlic powder
- Lemon wedges, for serving

SPICY LEMON GARLIC BUTTER

- ½ cup unsalted butter
- 4 cloves garlic, finely minced
- 1 teaspoon crushed red pepper flakes (adjust to heat level)
- Zest of 1 lemon
- Juice of 1 lemon (about 2 tablespoons)
- 1 tablespoon hot sauce (Melinda's Garlic Habanero or your favorite)
- 1 tablespoon chopped parsley

PREP THE GRILL: Fire up your grill to medium-high, around 400°F. Clean and oil those grates so the fish slides right off.

SEASON THE HALIBUT: Pat the fillets dry so they sear clean. Brush with olive oil and hit them with salt, pepper, paprika, and garlic powder. Let them chill for 10 minutes while you melt that butter magic.

MAKE THE SPICY LEMON GARLIC BUTTER: Melt butter in a small pan over medium heat. Add garlic and red pepper flakes and cook until fragrant, about a minute. Stir in lemon zest, lemon juice, hot sauce, and salt. Kill the heat and toss in the parsley. Keep it warm.

GRILL TIME: Lay the halibut on the grill, skin-side down if it has skin. Cook 3 to 4 minutes per side until lightly charred and flaky. Don't overdo it. Halibut cooks fast and you want it juicy.

FINISH WITH FLAVOR: Pull it off the grill and drown it in that spicy lemon garlic butter while it's hot. Let it soak for a minute before serving.

SERVE & SHINE: Plate it up with a squeeze of lemon, drizzle of extra butter, and sprinkle of parsley. Pairs perfectly with grilled veggies, rice, or a cold glass of white wine.

FLAVOR BOOST: Before grilling, brush the halibut with a thin coat of Dijon mustard mixed with a splash of lemon juice and your favorite hot sauce. That little layer helps the seasoning stick and adds a sneaky tang that wakes everything up.

DIXXON

CHAPTER 5

RIBS

TRACKSIDE RACKS

This chapter is dedicated to the crown jewel of any smoke session: pork ribs. From saucy baby backs to smoky St. Louis cuts, *Trackside Racks* is where that slow-smoked finger-food magic happens. We're talkin' bark that bites, meat that melts, and glazes that'll have you going crazy. From classic recipes to off-the-wall carnival eats and global-inspired bites. If you like pork on a stick, this chapter is for you. Buckle up, it's about to get wild.

Racks That Smack!

Corn Dog Ribs

This is backyard BBQ gone wild. Smoked baby backs get deboned, skewered, and dunked in a buttermilk cornbread batter before hitting the fryer for a golden, crispy finish. This is like State Fair meets backyard BBQ. It took over the internet, let them take over your life.

SERVES: 4 TO 6

PREP TIME: 30 MINUTES (AFTER RIBS ARE COOKED AND COOLED)

RIB SMOKE AND COOL TIME: 5 TO 6 HOURS

FRY TIME: 2 TO 3 MINUTES PER CORN DOG

TOTAL TIME: ABOUT 6 HOURS

RIBS

One 2½-to-3-pound rack baby back ribs

2 tablespoons yellow mustard (binder)

3 tablespoons SPG+ Rub (page 30) or your favorite

¼ cup apple juice or spritz of choice (beer, water, or apple cider vinegar and water mix)

2 tablespoons unsalted butter, cut into small pieces

2 tablespoons brown sugar

2 tablespoons honey

BBQ SAUCE

½ cup ketchup

½ cup Coca-Cola

1 tablespoon Worcestershire sauce

2 tablespoons honey

1 tablespoon your favorite BBQ rub

MUSTARD CORN DOG SAUCE

2 tablespoons yellow mustard

2 tablespoons mayonnaise

1 teaspoon honey

½ teaspoon hot sauce (optional)

SMOKING THE RIBS: Remove the membrane from the bone side of the ribs. Rub the ribs with mustard and coat evenly with 2 to 3 tablespoons SPG+ Rub.

Preheat your smoker to 250°F. Place the ribs bone-side down on the smoker grate. Smoke unwrapped for 2½ to 3 hours, spritzing with apple juice (or spritz of choice) every 45 minutes after the first hour.

Lay out a large piece of heavy-duty foil. Place the ribs meat-side down on a sheet of heavy-duty foil. Top with the butter pieces, brown sugar, and honey. Wrap tightly and return to the smoker. Continue cooking for another 90 minutes to 2 hours, or until the internal temperature reaches 202°F to 205°F and they are very tender.

Let the ribs rest, unwrapped, for 10 to 20 minutes until cool enough to handle. Carefully remove all the bones from the rack while trying to keep the meat slab as intact as possible.

Let the deboned rib meat cool completely (chilling it can make slicing easier). Once cooled, use the grooves where the bones were as a guide to slice the meat into individual "riblets." Insert a wooden skewer or ice pop stick into each riblet.

Prepare the sauces while the ribs rest and cool:

BBQ SAUCE: Combine the ketchup, Coca-Cola, Worcestershire sauce, honey, and rub in a small saucepan. Simmer over medium-low heat for 10 to 15 minutes, stirring occasionally, until thickened.

MUSTARD CORN DOG SAUCE: In a small bowl, mix together the yellow mustard, mayonnaise, honey, and hot sauce, if using, until smooth. Set aside.

CONTINUED

FOR FRYING

Neutral oil (canola, vegetable, or peanut) for deep frying

CORNBREAD BATTER

1 cup yellow cornmeal

1 cup all-purpose flour

1 tablespoon granulated sugar

1 teaspoon baking powder

½ teaspoon kosher salt

1 cup buttermilk

1 large egg

1 tablespoon yellow mustard

1 tablespoon hot sauce (optional)

FRYING THE RIB CORN DOGS: Heat 2 to 3 inches neutral oil in a deep fryer or a heavy-bottomed pot over medium heat to 350°F.

MAKE THE BATTER: In a large bowl, whisk together the cornmeal, flour, granulated sugar, baking powder, and salt. In a separate bowl, whisk together the buttermilk, egg, yellow mustard, and hot sauce, if using. Pour the wet ingredients into the dry ingredients and mix until just smooth (a few small lumps are okay). Let the batter rest for 10 minutes. (Transferring the batter to a tall glass can make dipping easier.)

Dip each skewered riblet into the batter, ensuring each is well coated. Allow any excess batter to drip off. Carefully place two or three battered riblets at a time into the hot oil. Fry for 2 to 3 minutes, turning occasionally, until golden brown and crisp. Remove from the oil and drain on a wire rack or paper towels.

SERVE: Serve the corn dog ribs hot with the prepared BBQ sauce and mustard corn dog sauce on the side for dipping, or drizzle over the top.

FLAVOR BOOST: As soon as the corn dogs ribs come out the fryer, brush 'em with warm BBQ sauce and dust with your rub while they're still sticky. That flavor boost takes 'em from "damn, that's good" to "where have these been all my life."

Argentine Open-Fire Ribs

My friend Al Frugoni put me onto Argentine-style open fire ribs, and I've been hooked ever since. They're my personal favorite way to eat ribs. Simple, pork forward, smoky, salty goodness cooked right over the flames. It's primal, it's delicious, and it's BBQ in its purest form. Shout-out to Al for leading the way!

SERVES: 4 TO 6

PREP TIME: 10 MINUTES PLUS TIME TO BUILD THE FIRE

COOK TIME: 3½ TO 4 HOURS

1 rack St. Louis-style spareribs

Extra-virgin olive oil, for coating

Kosher salt and freshly ground black pepper

EQUIPMENT

Open fire pit, Santa Maria grill, or grill with open fire indirect capability

Grill grate that can be positioned 18 to 24 inches from hot coals

Hardwood (oak, mesquite, apple, or cherry)

PREP THE RIBS: Leave the membrane on. It will protect the ribs and also crisp up during cooking. Lightly coat both sides of the rib rack with olive oil. Season *generously* with salt and a kiss of pepper on all sides. You want enough salt to help form a bit of a crust as the ribs cook and the fat renders and just enough pepper to make it pop. Let the ribs sit at room temperature while you build and prepare your fire.

BUILD THE FIRE: Start a fire with your chosen hardwood. Allow the wood to burn down until you have a substantial bed of hot coals. You are looking for radiant heat, not active flames licking the grill grate.

Position your grill grate 18 to 24 inches above the heat source (the bed of coals). You want a steady, medium-low to medium heat. You should be able to hold your hand at grill level for 5 to 7 seconds before it gets too hot. Arrange the coals to one side for indirect cooking if your setup allows, or ensure an even bed if cooking directly over them but at a significant height.

START COOKING: Place the seasoned rib rack on the grill grate, bone-side down. If cooking indirectly, place the rack away from the direct concentration of coals. Cook slow and steady for 3 to 3½ hours. The goal is to let the heat from the coals gently cook the ribs, render the fat, and allow the salt to work its magic. Maintain a consistent fire by adding small pieces of wood or pre-burned coals as needed to keep the heat steady. Avoid large flare-ups. Do not flip the ribs during this initial long cook. The bones will protect the meat from drying out.

DO THE FINAL FLIP (MEAT-SIDE DOWN): After 3 to 3½ hours, the ribs should be well rendered, nicely browned on the bone side, and the meat should be tender. For the last 20 to 30 minutes of cooking, carefully flip the rib rack meat-side down, directly exposed to the heat. This step is crucial for crisping up the fat on the meat side and adding deep caramelization. Watch the ribs closely during this phase to prevent burning. The ribs should have a nice bite when finished.

REST AND SLICE: Remove the ribs from the grill once the meat side is beautifully browned and crisped.

Let the rack rest, tented loosely with foil, if desired, for about 10 minutes before slicing. Slice between the bones and serve immediately.

BOSS MOVE

While the ribs rest, brush on a little beef tallow or hot bacon fat, then crack fresh black pepper over the top. It revives the crust, adds rich shine, and makes the bark pop like a cast-iron rib eye.

Al Pastor Ribs

These ribs don't just please, they preach. Not traditional al pastor, but the flavor hits all the same notes and these ribs smack. Wrapped around a pineapple, smoked low and slow, and glazed in smoky-sweet, fiery goodness. They baste themselves in pineapple juice till sticky, tender, and straight-up ridiculous. They look wild on the smoker, but taste even better.

SERVES: 4 TO 6

PREP TIME: 15 MINUTES (PLUS 30 MINUTES RUB REST, OR OVERNIGHT REFRIGERATION)

COOK TIME: 3½ TO 4 HOURS

SIMPLE AL PASTOR RUB

2 tablespoons chili powder (preferably ancho or a mild blend)

1 tablespoon smoked paprika

1 tablespoon brown sugar

1 teaspoon garlic powder

1 teaspoon ground cumin

1 teaspoon kosher salt

½ teaspoon freshly ground black pepper

RIBS

1 rack baby back or St. Louis–style ribs, membrane removed

1 large whole pineapple, ripe, but firm

AL PASTOR GLAZE

¼ cup pineapple juice (from the cored pineapple or canned)

2 tablespoons honey

½ tablespoon chipotle powder

1 tablespoon apple cider vinegar

1 tablespoon achiote paste or rub

Pinch of kosher salt

FOR SERVING

Chopped fresh pineapple or cored and smoked pineapple

Lime wedges

Chopped fresh cilantro (optional)

PREP THE RIBS AND PINEAPPLE: In a small bowl, mix together the rub ingredients. Coat the rack with your rub. Let it sit at room temperature for at least 30 minutes, or cover and refrigerate for up to overnight to let the flavors penetrate.

PREPARE THE PINEAPPLE: Peel the pineapple. Trim the top (leafy crown) and bottom so they are flat and stable. You can core the pineapple if desired or leave it whole.

ASSEMBLE THE RIBS: Wrap your slab of baby back ribs around the pineapple. Using long metal skewers (or wooden skewers that have been soaked in water for at least 30 minutes), secure the rack of ribs to the pineapple. Pierce the skewers through the meat and then into the pineapple.

SMOKE THE RIBS: Preheat your smoker to 250°F. Use a fruitwood like apple or cherry, or a blend that complements pork. Carefully place the entire pineapple-rib tower onto the smoker grates. You can smoke on a rack/cooking pan if easier. Smoke for 3½ to 4 hours, or until the ribs are tender and reach an internal temperature of 185°F to 190°F. The pineapple will also cook and release juices, basting the ribs.

MAKE THE AL PASTOR GLAZE: While the ribs are smoking (about 30 minutes before they are done), prepare the glaze. In a small saucepan, combine all the glaze ingredients. Bring to a simmer over medium-low heat and cook for 5 to 7 minutes, stirring occasionally, until the glaze has slightly thickened.

GLAZE AND FINISH: During the final 10 to 15 minutes of smoking, brush the al pastor glaze generously all over the ribs. Allow the heat of the smoker to caramelize the glaze slightly.

REST AND SERVE: Carefully remove the ribs from the smoker. Let them rest for about 10 minutes. Remove the skewers and take the ribs off the pineapple. Chop the pineapple into pieces. Serve the ribs with pineapple, lime wedges for squeezing, and a sprinkle of cilantro, if desired.

BOSS MOVE

Right before glazing, blend some of that smoked pineapple into the glaze for extra caramelized sweetness. After slicing, drizzle the warm glaze and toss on chopped grilled pineapple. It's juicy-on-juicy flavor that's a real sweet treat!

The Classic Rack

These ribs are the backyard anthem. Simple, smoky, and always a hit. Like that classic track you never skip, they're nostalgic, easy, and flat-out delicious every time. Perfect if you're just getting your feet wet on the smoker, and still the kind of recipe you'll keep coming back to once you're a seasoned vet.

SERVES: 2 TO 3
PREP TIME: 15 MINUTES
COOK TIME: 5 TO 6 HOURS
TOTAL TIME: 5 HOURS 15 MINUTES TO 6 HOURS 15 MINUTES

RIBS

One 2½-to-3-pound rack baby back or St. Louis-style ribrack

1 tablespoon yellow mustard or neutral oil

RUB

1 tablespoon kosher salt

1 tablespoon freshly ground black pepper

½ tablespoon paprika (optional, for color)

FOR SMOKING

Apple, cherry, pecan, or your favorite mild fruitwood

SPRITZ (OPTIONAL)

Water, apple juice, light beer, 50/50 mix of apple cider vinegar and water, or chicken broth.

½ cup BBQ sauce of your choice

PREP THE RIBS: Locate the thin membrane on the bone side of the ribs. Using a butter knife or your fingers, gently lift a corner of the membrane before gripping it with a paper towel and pulling it off completely. This step is optional but I recommend it for this recipe. Rub the entire rack of ribs (both sides) with the yellow mustard or neutral oil to act as a binder for the seasoning.

SEASON THE RIBS: In a small bowl, mix together the salt, pepper, and paprika, if using. Sprinkle this seasoning blend evenly over both sides of the ribs, patting it gently into the meat.

PREHEAT THE SMOKER: Preheat your smoker to 250°F. Add a chunk or a small handful of your chosen smoking wood to the fire or smoker box according to your smoker's instructions.

SMOKE THE RIBS: Place the seasoned ribs bone-side down directly on the smoker grates. Smoke at 250°F for 4½ to 5½ hours, or until the ribs have a deep mahogany color and pass the "bend test" (when you pick up the rack with tongs from one end, it should flex easily and the surface should crack slightly, but the meat should not fall apart).

SPRITZING NOTE: After the first 2 hours of smoking, spritz the ribs every 45 to 60 minutes if they start to look dry. Use a food-safe spray bottle and lightly mist with your chosen spritz liquid. This helps keep the ribs moist and can contribute to bark formation and flavor.

SAUCE AND SET: During the last 30 minutes of the smoking process, brush both sides of the ribs generously with your favorite BBQ sauce. Continue to cook until the sauce has set and become tacky, but not burnt.

REST AND SERVE: Remove the ribs from the smoker and let them rest, tented loosely with foil, for about 10 minutes before slicing. Slice the rack between the bones and serve immediately.

BOSS MOVE

After the final glaze, hit the ribs with warm butter, a splash of cider vinegar, and a touch of honey. Guaranteed to give your ribs the proper finish.

Coca-Cola Ribs

When I think backyard BBQ, this is the recipe that comes to mind. These Coke-glazed ribs went viral for a reason: They're simple, bold, and packed with flavor. Coke works double here in the marinade and the sauce. Hit 'em with SPG, smoke low and slow, and let that sweet glaze do its thing. No wrap, no stress, just good smoke, cold drinks, and ribs that disappear fast.

SERVES: 2 TO 3

MARINATE TIME: 4 TO 6 HOURS OR OVERNIGHT

PREP TIME (AFTER MARINATING): 20 MINUTES

COOK TIME: 4½ TO 5 HOURS

RIBS

One 2½-to-3-pound rack baby back or St. Louis-style ribs

Two 12-ounce cans Coca-Cola

FOR SMOKING

Mild fruitwood such as cherry, apple, or pecan

SPG RUB

1 tablespoon kosher salt

1 tablespoon freshly ground black pepper

1 tablespoon garlic powder

SPRITZ (OPTIONAL)

Apple juice, water, or a mix of Coke and apple cider vinegar

COCA-COLA BBQ SAUCE

1 cup Coca-Cola

¾ cup ketchup

1½ tablespoons Worcestershire sauce

2 tablespoons honey

1 tablespoon of your favorite BBQ rub (something sweet-savory with a kick)

MARINATE THE RIBS: Remove the membrane from the bone side of the ribs. Place the ribs in a large zip-top bag or a shallow, non-reactive container. Pour the Coca-Cola over the ribs, ensuring they are fully submerged. Seal the bag or cover the container and marinate in the refrigerator for 4 to 6 hours, or preferably overnight for maximum flavor penetration.

PREHEAT YOUR SMOKER: Preheat your smoker to 250°F using a mild wood like cherry, apple, or pecan.

DRY AND SEASON THE RIBS: Make the SPG rub: In a small bowl, stir together the salt, pepper, and garlic powder. Remove the ribs from the Coca-Cola marinade; discard the marinade. Pat the ribs completely dry with paper towels. Season both sides of the ribs generously with the SPG rub. Let the ribs sit at room temperature for 15 to 20 minutes to allow the rub to "sweat" and adhere to the meat.

SMOKE THE RIBS: Place the seasoned ribs meat-side up on the smoker grates. Smoke at 250°F for 3½ to 4 hours, or until the meat starts to pull back from the ends of the bones by about ½ inch and a toothpick or probe slides into the meat between the bones with little resistance.

SPRITZ (OPTIONAL): After the first 2 hours of smoking, if the ribs start to look dry, spritz them every 30 to 45 minutes with apple juice, water, or a mixture of Coca-Cola and apple cider vinegar.

MAKE THE COCA-COLA BBQ SAUCE: While the ribs are smoking, prepare the glaze. In a medium saucepan over medium heat, combine the Coca-Cola, ketchup, Worcestershire sauce, honey, and your favorite BBQ rub. Bring the mixture to a simmer and cook for 12 to 15 minutes, stirring occasionally, until it has thickened to a glossy glaze consistency. Set aside.

GLAZE AND FINISH: During the last 20 to 30 minutes of the smoking process, brush the ribs generously on all sides with your prepared Coca-Cola BBQ sauce. Allow the sauce to set and become tacky in the smoker.

REST AND SERVE: Remove the ribs from the smoker and let them rest, tented loosely with foil, for about 10 minutes before slicing. Slice between the bones and serve with any extra Coca-Cola BBQ sauce on the side.

BOSS MOVE

Add a splash of bourbon to your Coke BBQ sauce while it simmers. It deepens the flavor, adds a subtle kick, and who doesn't like a little booze with their BBQ?

The Ribwich

This is the rib sandwich McDonald's wishes it had. Those ain't even real ribs, but these right here are the truth. Smoky, saucy, and stacked high with flavor dripping like a leaky faucet. Pull up with this and everyone at the party's gonna be talking. You could share it, but let's be real . . . you won't want to.

SERVES: 4 HUNGRY FOLKS
PREP TIME: 20 MINUTES
COOK TIME: 5 TO 6 HOURS
TOTAL TIME: 5 HOURS 20 MINUTES TO 6 HOURS 20 MINUTES

RIBS

One 2½-to-3-pound rack St. Louis–style pork spareribs

2 tablespoons yellow mustard

3 to 4 tablespoons of your favorite sweet and smoky BBQ rub

FOR SMOKING

Wood: Hickory or cherry preferred

Mix of apple juice and water or light beer, for spritzing (optional)

Splash of apple juice or a few pats of unsalted butter (optional)

FOR ASSEMBLY

1 large French baguette or sourdough baguette, about 24 inches long

Unsalted butter, at room temperature, for toasting

¼ cup mayonnaise (Duke's or Kewpie recommended)

½ to ¾ cup of your favorite BBQ sauce

½ medium white onion, very thinly sliced

12 to 16 dill pickle chips or sandwich slices

PREP THE RIBS: Remove the membrane from the bone side of the ribs. Pat the ribs dry, then rub with the yellow mustard to act as a binder. Season thoroughly on all sides with your favorite BBQ rub. Let the ribs sit at room temperature while you fire up the smoker.

SMOKE THE RIBS (UNWRAPPED): Preheat your smoker to 250°F. Add hickory or cherry wood for smoking.

Place the ribs bone-side down on the smoker grates. Smoke for 3 hours. If using a spritz, lightly mist the ribs every 45 to 60 minutes after the first hour if they appear to be drying out.

WRAP AND BRAISE: After 3 hours of smoking, remove the ribs. Lay them on a large sheet of heavy-duty aluminum foil. Add a splash of apple juice or a few pats of butter on top of the meat, if desired. Wrap the ribs tightly in the foil. Return the wrapped ribs to the smoker for another 2 hours, or until they are probe-tender and achieve an internal temperature of 195°F to 203°F.

DEBONE THE RIBS: Carefully unwrap the ribs (be mindful of hot steam). Let them rest for about 20 minutes, or until cool enough to handle but still warm. Gently remove all the bones from the slab. The meat should be tender enough for the bones to pull out cleanly, ideally keeping the slab of meat intact.

TOAST THE BAGUETTE: Slice the baguette lengthwise, but not all the way through, so it opens like a book. Spread a thin layer of butter on the cut insides of the baguette. Toast the buttered insides on a grill, griddle, or in a large pan until golden brown and crisp.

ASSEMBLE THE RIBWICH: Spread the mayonnaise evenly on both toasted insides of the baguette. Carefully lay the deboned rib slab onto the bottom half of the baguette. Drizzle or brush the rib meat generously with BBQ sauce. Top with the onion and dill pickle chips or slices. Close the sandwich with the top half of the baguette. You can slice the large sandwich into four massive servings.

FLAVOR BOOST: For a melty version, add cheese when assembling, wrap the sandwich tightly in foil, then place it back on the smoker for 10 to 15 minutes.

Lemon Pepper Ribs

Pork and lemon go together like Jordan and Pippen, and this recipe proves it. Bright, bold, and buttery with a peppery kick that keeps you reaching for "just one more." Perfect for backyard hangs when you want flavor that dunks right on your taste buds.

SERVES: 4
PREP TIME: 15 MINUTES
COOK TIME: ABOUT 5 HOURS

RIBS

1 rack baby back or St. Louis–style ribs

Yellow mustard, for a binder (optional)

2 tablespoons Lemon Pepper Herb Rub (page 31)

WRAP

2 tablespoons unsalted butter, cut into pats

2 tablespoons freshly squeezed lemon juice

1 tablespoon honey

LEMON PEPPER GLAZE

¼ cup freshly squeezed lemon juice

2 tablespoons honey

½ tablespoon Lemon Pepper Herb Rub (page 31)

1 tablespoon unsalted butter

1 teaspoon lemon zest

1 teaspoon freshly ground black pepper

Pinch of kosher salt

PREP THE RIBS: Remove the membrane from the bone side of your rack (optional). Apply a light coat of yellow mustard to act as a binder, if using. Generously coat the ribs on all sides with the lemon pepper rub, patting it into the meat.

SMOKE THE RIBS (UNWRAPPED): Preheat your smoker to 250°F using indirect heat. Use a mild fruitwood like apple or cherry. Place the seasoned ribs bone-side down directly on the smoker grates. Smoke unwrapped for about 3 hours, or until a good bark has formed and the ribs have taken on a nice reddish-mahogany color.

WRAP THE RIBS: Lay out two large sheets of heavy-duty aluminum foil. Place the rack meat-side down on a sheet of foil. Top the bone side with the butter and drizzle with the lemon juice, and honey. Wrap tightly in its foil packet, ensuring a good seal. Return the wrapped ribs to the smoker (meat-side down inside the foil). Continue to cook for another 1½ to 2 hours, or until the ribs are tender.

MAKE THE LEMON PEPPER GLAZE: In a small saucepan, combine the ingredients for the glaze. Bring the mixture to a simmer over medium-low heat. Cook for 5 to 7 minutes, stirring occasionally, until the glaze has slightly thickened and the flavors have melded. Remove from the heat.

FINISH AND GLAZE THE RIBS: Carefully unwrap the ribs from the foil (be cautious of hot steam). Discard the foil and any accumulated liquid. Brush the ribs on all sides with the prepared lemon pepper glaze.

Return the glazed ribs, unwrapped, to the smoker for another 15 to 20 minutes to allow the glaze to set and become tacky.

REST AND SERVE: Remove the ribs from the smoker and let them rest for 5 to 10 minutes before slicing. Slice between the bones.

BOSS MOVE

Right after glazing, grate fresh Parm over the ribs so it melts into the bark. That salty umami punch goes crazy with the lemon-pepper combo. For an extra pop of flavor and presentation, you can hit them with a fresh grind of black pepper and some lemon juice before serving.

Salsa Verde Ribs

These ribs are pure flavor magic. Braised in a bold homemade salsa verde with roasted tomatillos, garlic, chiles, and lime until they're fall-apart tender and dripping in green gold. It's low-and-slow BBQ colliding with Mexican soul food, and the kind of recipe that'll get you invited to every carne asada.

SERVES: 4 TO 6
PREP TIME: 30 MINUTES
COOK TIME: 2½ TO 3 HOURS (90-MINUTE SMOKE PLUS 60 TO 90 MINUTES SIMMER)

RIBS

One 3-to-3½-pound rack pork spareribs or baby back ribs

2 tablespoons yellow mustard or hot sauce

3 tablespoons pork rub or your favorite seasoning blend

FOR SMOKING

Hickory, oak, or even something fruity like apple or cherry; mix and match if you're feeling wild!

SALSA VERDE

1½ pounds tomatillos, husks removed and rinsed

8 large cloves garlic, peeled

1 medium yellow onion, quartered

2 jalapeño or serrano chiles, stems removed (seeded for less heat or not for more heat)

4 green onions, trimmed (white and light-green parts)

Extra-virgin olive oil, for roasting

½ cup fresh cilantro, coarsely chopped (stems are fine)

¼ cup freshly squeezed lime juice (2 limes), plus more as needed

1 teaspoon ground cumin

1 teaspoon dried Mexican oregano or regular oregano

1 cup low-sodium chicken broth

Kosher salt

GARNISH

Cotija cheese

Chopped fresh cilantro

Lime wedges

Warm tortillas, rice, or charro beans, for serving

PREP THE RIBS: Remove the membrane from the bone side of the ribs and pat them dry. If desired, slice the rack between the bones to create individual ribs (this helps them submerge better in the sauce later, but you can also leave the rack whole). Rub the ribs all over with yellow mustard or hot sauce to act as a binder. Generously coat all sides of the ribs with pork rub. Let the ribs rest at room temperature while your smoker preheats.

SMOKE THE RIBS: Preheat your smoker to 275°F. Place the seasoned ribs directly on the smoker grates. Smoke for 90 minutes, until a good bark is starting to set and the ribs have taken on a nice smoky color.

MAKE THE *SALSA VERDE*: While the ribs are smoking, preheat your oven to 425°F (or prepare your grill for direct high heat). On a baking sheet, toss the tomatillos, garlic cloves, yellow onion, jalapeños, and green onions with a light drizzle of olive oil.

Roast the vegetables for 15 to 20 minutes, or until they are blistered, softened, and slightly charred.

Transfer the roasted vegetables and any accumulated juices to a blender. Add the cilantro, lime juice, cumin, oregano, low-sodium chicken broth, and a good pinch of salt. Blend until the sauce is smooth but still has some texture. Taste and adjust the seasoning with more salt or lime juice as needed.

SIMMER THE RIBS: Once the ribs have smoked for 90 minutes, transfer them to a deep pot, Dutch oven, or a deep foil pan. Pour the prepared *salsa verde* over the ribs, ensuring they are mostly covered by the sauce. Cover the pot or pan tightly. Simmer gently over low to medium-low heat on the stovetop (or you can return to the smoker at a lower temp around 250°F or place in a 300°F oven) for 60 to 90 minutes. The ribs should be tender but not completely falling apart.

OPTIONAL: For a thicker sauce, uncover the pot during the last 10 to 15 minutes of simmering to allow some of the liquid to evaporate.

SERVE: Remove the ribs from the *salsa verde* and plate with plenty of sauce. Garnish with Cotija, cilantro, and lime wedges. Serve with warm tortillas, rice, or beans.

BOSS MOVE

Right before serving, char some of that salsa verde under the broiler or in a cast-iron pan to add a smoky, roasted edge. Then spoon it hot over the ribs and continue serving like you would.

Dr Pepper Sticky Ribs

These ribs go from zero to outrageous real quick. Smoked until tender, fried until crispy, then tossed in a sticky, sweet Dr Pepper glaze that clings like a BBQ boss. My friend Stephen loves Dr Pepper. He said if I cared about him, I'd make Dr Pepper ribs. I did. And they're insanely good.

SERVES: 2 TO 4
PREP TIME: 30 MINUTES
MARINATE TIME: 2 TO 4 HOURS
SMOKE TIME: ABOUT 90 MINUTES
TOTAL TIME (EXCLUDING MARINATING): ABOUT 2 HOURS

RIBS AND MARINADE

1 rack baby back ribs, membrane removed, cut into individual bones

One 12-ounce can Dr Pepper

1 tablespoon soy sauce

1 tablespoon hot sauce (optional)

1 tablespoon Worcestershire sauce

1½ tablespoons of your favorite BBQ rub (for the marinade)

2 tablespoons AP BBQ Rub (page 30)

FOR SMOKING

Mild fruitwood like apple or cherry

DR PEPPER GLAZE

¾ cup Dr Pepper

⅓ cup ketchup

2 tablespoons honey

1 tablespoon soy sauce

1 tablespoon of your favorite BBQ rub

FRY COATING

1 cup all-purpose flour

½ cup rice flour or cornstarch for extra crunch

1 teaspoon kosher salt

½ teaspoons freshly ground black pepper

1 teaspoon garlic powder

FOR FRYING

Neutral oil (canola, peanut, or vegetable)

MARINATE THE RIBS: In a large zip-top bag or a non-reactive bowl, combine the cut rib bones, Dr Pepper, soy sauce, hot sauce, if using, Worcestershire sauce, and your favorite BBQ rub. Ensure the ribs are well coated. Seal the bag (pressing out excess air) or cover the bowl. Marinate in the refrigerator for 2 to 4 hours.

SMOKE THE RIBS: Preheat your smoker to 275°F. Remove the ribs from the marinade, discarding the marinade, and pat them dry with paper towels. Season the ribs on all sides with the AP BBQ rub. Place the seasoned ribs directly on the smoker grate. Smoke for approximately 90 minutes, or until the ribs reach an internal temperature of 165°F to 175°F and have developed a deep, smoky color. Let the smoked ribs cool for 10 to 15 minutes before proceeding to frying. They should be cool enough to handle.

MAKE THE DR PEPPER GLAZE: In a small saucepan, combine the Dr Pepper, ketchup, honey, soy sauce, and BBQ rub. Bring the mixture to a boil over medium heat, then reduce to a simmer. Simmer for 10 to 12 minutes, stirring occasionally, or until the glaze has thickened to a syrupy consistency and is glossy. Keep warm.

FRY THE RIBS: In a large bowl, whisk together the flour, rice flour (or cornstarch), salt, the pepper, and garlic powder for the fry coating. Toss the cooled, smoked ribs in the flour mixture until evenly and thoroughly coated. Shake off any excess flour.

Heat 2 to 3 inches of neutral oil in a deep fryer or a large, heavy-bottomed Dutch oven over medium to medium-high heat to 350°F.

Carefully place the floured ribs into the hot oil, frying in batches to avoid overcrowding the pot. Fry for 3 to 4 minutes, turning occasionally, until the coating is golden brown and very crispy. Remove the fried ribs with a slotted spoon or tongs and drain on a wire rack.

TOSS AND SERVE: Place the hot, crispy fried ribs in a large clean bowl. Pour the warm Dr Pepper glaze over the ribs and toss gently until they are fully coated and glistening. Serve immediately.

FLAVOR BOOST: Dust those ribs with a little extra BBQ rub *after* the glaze while they're still hot. It'll stick to the saucy surface and punch up the flavor with every bite. Serve 'em with a side of ranch for dipping. Trust me.

Smoked Chicken-Fried Ribs

These ribs are what happens after I have a couple beverages. They're like the best damn piece of fried chicken you've ever had . . . except it's a rib. Crunchy, juicy, smoky, and smothered . . . this dish doesn't just bring the heat, it burns the house down.

SERVES: 4 TO 6
SMOKE TIME: 3 TO 4 HOURS
COOK TIME: 4 TO 6 HOURS
TOTAL TIME (EXCLUDING BUTTERMILK MARINATING): 4 TO 5 HOURS

RIBS

1 rack St. Louis-style ribs or pork spareribs

Yellow mustard or hot sauce, for coating

Your favorite BBQ rub (enough to coat generously)

Kosher salt and freshly ground black pepper (optional, depending on the rub)

DREDGE AND MARINADE

2 cups buttermilk

2 teaspoons hot sauce (such as Bear & Burton's Special Reserve or Melinda's)

2 cups all-purpose flour

½ cup cornstarch (for extra crispiness)

2 tablespoons of your favorite spicy BBQ rub

Kosher salt

FOR FRYING

Peanut oil or other neutral high-heat oil

COUNTRY GRAVY

1 thick strip smoked bacon

Unsalted butter or neutral oil, as needed

3 tablespoons all-purpose flour

2½ cups whole milk, warmed

1 teaspoon freshly ground black pepper, plus more as needed

Kosher salt

Pinch of ground sage, cayenne pepper, or a dash of hot sauce, for extra depth (optional)

SMOKE THE RIBS: Preheat smoker to 250°F. Remove the membrane and coat ribs with mustard or hot sauce as a binder. Season all sides generously with BBQ rub and a little salt and pepper. Smoke 3 to 4 hours, until tender but not falling apart (they need to hold for frying). Rest 5 minutes, then slice into individual bones.

MARINATE IN BUTTERMILK: Whisk the buttermilk with the hot sauce. Submerge the ribs, cover, and refrigerate at least 1 hour or overnight to tenderize.

DREDGE AND REST: In a shallow bowl, mix the flour, cornstarch, and BBQ rub. Add salt if needed. Dip the ribs from the buttermilk into the flour mix, then back into the buttermilk, then flour again for that double dredge. Set on a wire rack for 15 to 20 minutes to help the coating stick.

FRY THE RIBS: Heat 2 to 3 inches of oil to 350°F. Fry ribs in batches for 3 to 4 minutes per side until crispy and golden. Drain on paper towels or a rack and sprinkle with salt or rub.

MAKE THE GRAVY: In a skillet, cook the bacon until crisp. Keep about 3 tablespoons of fat in the pan. Add the flour and whisk for 1 to 2 minutes to make a roux. Slowly whisk in the warm milk, stirring until smooth and thickened. Season with salt, pepper, and a touch of sage, cayenne, or hot sauce. Stir in or top with crumbled bacon.

SERVE: Stack the crispy ribs, smother with that peppery bacon gravy, and finish with extra bacon or a sprinkle of rub if you're feeling bold.

BOSS MOVE

Drizzle the maple syrup over those crispy fried ribs before the the gravy. That sweet hit cuts the richness and gives you a chicken-and-waffles vibe with a Southern BBQ twist with brunch vibes.

Cotton Candy Ribs

These came to me one day while I was up in the clouds, for lack of a better word. It sounded crazy, but I had to try it. Somehow, it actually worked. The cotton candy crust is legitimately mind-blowing. And then there's the Hot Cheetos to finish... something even Willy Wonka wouldn't have dreamed up. These ribs are fun to make, and even more fun to eat.

SERVES: 4 TO 6
PREP TIME: 15 MINUTES
COOK TIME: ABOUT 5 HOURS
TOTAL TIME: ABOUT 5 HOURS 15 MINUTES

RIBS

1 rack baby back ribs

1 tablespoon yellow mustard (optional)

2 tablespoons Sweet Heat Island Rub (page 31) or your favorite

Splash of root beer (optional)

FOR SMOKING

Mild fruitwood like apple or cherry

ROOT BEER GLAZE

1 cup of your favorite sweet BBQ sauce

½ cup root beer (regular, not diet)

2 tablespoons hot sauce (something tangy with a little heat, such as Frank's RedHot or Cholula)

¼ cup packed brown sugar

2 tablespoons unsalted butter

FOR FINISHING

1 to 2 cups pink or blue cotton candy

½ cup crushed Flamin' Hot Cheetos

PREP THE RIBS: Remove the membrane from the ribs if you'd like. Rub the rack all over with a thin, even coat of yellow mustard to act as a binder for the rub. Generously coat both sides of the ribs with your favorite sweet heat rub. Let the seasoned ribs sit at room temperature while you fire up the smoker.

SMOKE LOW AND SLOW (UNWRAPPED): Preheat your smoker to 250°F. Place the ribs bone-side down directly on the smoker grates. Smoke uncovered for 3 hours.

WRAP AND TENDERIZE: After 3 hours, remove the ribs from the smoker. Lay out a sheet of heavy-duty aluminum foil. Lay your rack of ribs in the center. If desired, add a small splash of root beer to the foil packet before sealing. Wrap the rack tightly in its foil packet. Return the wrapped ribs to the smoker and continue to cook for another 2 hours, or until they are tender but still holding their shape (they should bend easily but not fall apart).

MAKE THE GLAZE: While the ribs are in the wrapped stage, prepare the glaze. In a medium saucepan, combine the BBQ sauce, root beer, hot sauce, brown sugar, and butter. Bring the mixture to a simmer over medium heat, then reduce the heat to low. Cook, stirring often, for 10 to 15 minutes, or until the glaze has reduced slightly and thickened to a syrupy consistency.

GLAZE AND FINISH SMOKING: Carefully unwrap the ribs from the foil (be cautious of hot steam). Discard the foil and any accumulated liquid. Brush the meat side of the ribs generously with the prepared glaze. Return the glazed ribs, unwrapped, to the smoker for another 15 to 20 minutes to allow the glaze to set and become tacky.

END WITH THE COTTON CANDY FINALE: Pull the glazed ribs off the smoker while they are still very hot. Working quickly, immediately top the hot ribs with a layer of cotton candy, covering the surface. The heat from the ribs will cause the cotton candy to melt and create a glossy, sticky candy shell.

SLICE AND TOP: Let the ribs sit for a minute or two for the cotton candy glaze to fully set. Just before slicing, sprinkle the ribs generously with crushed Flamin' Hot Cheetos for a crunchy, spicy contrast. Slice and serve.

BOSS MOVE

After you pile the cotton candy on top of the ribs, tent them with foil and hit it with a torch or slide the whole rack into a hot oven for a minute. The heat melts the sugar down fast, wrapping the ribs in an insane candy crust that'll have you thinking you just bit into pork flavored pop rocks!

Christmas Ribs

These ribs are my way of bringing holiday vibes straight from the grill. Juicy ribs get hit with a sweet and tangy pomegranate chimichurri that's as colorful as it is flavorful. The bright reds and greens will have you thinking Christmas right away, and the taste? Like unwrapping a present for your mouth. Festive, bold, and delicious.

SERVES: 4 TO 6
PREP TIME: 25 MINUTES
COOK TIME: 4 TO 5½ HOURS

RIBS

1 rack baby back or St. Louis-style pork ribs

1 tablespoon fish sauce (optional)

SIMPLE RUB

1½ tablespoons kosher salt

1 tablespoon freshly ground black pepper

½ tablespoon granulated garlic or garlic powder

Splash of apple cider vinegar or pomegranate juice (optional)

POMEGRANATE CHIMICHURRI

½ cup pomegranate seeds

½ cup finely chopped fresh cilantro

¼ cup finely chopped fresh flat-leaf parsley

¼ cup finely chopped red onion

3 cloves garlic, finely minced

1 small red chile or Fresno pepper, seeded (for less heat) and finely chopped (optional)

2 tablespoons red wine vinegar

2 tablespoons freshly squeezed lime juice (1 lime)

½ cup extra-virgin olive oil

Kosher salt and freshly ground black pepper

PREP THE RIBS: Remove the membrane from the bone side of the ribs. Rub the ribs with fish sauce, if using. In a small bowl, combine the salt, pepper, and granulated garlic. Season the ribs generously on all sides with this simple rub.

SMOKE THE RIBS (UNWRAPPED): Preheat your smoker to 250°F to 275°F. Place the ribs bone-side down directly on the smoker grates. Smoke uncovered for about 3 hours, or until a good bark has formed and the ribs have taken on a deep color.

WRAP (OPTIONAL, FOR EXTRA TENDERNESS): After 3 hours, if the bark is well set and you prefer very tender, fall-off-the-bone-style ribs, you can wrap them. Lay out a sheet of heavy-duty aluminum foil. Place the rack of ribs in the center. Add a small splash of apple cider vinegar or pomegranate juice to the foil packet before sealing, if you like. Wrap the rack tightly in its foil.

Return the wrapped ribs to the smoker and continue to cook for another 1½ to 2 hours, or until they are probe-tender. If you prefer ribs with more bite, you can skip the wrapping step and continue to cook them unwrapped until tender, which will likely be 4½ to 5 hours total.

MAKE THE POMEGRANATE CHIMICHURRI: While the ribs are finishing their cook (or while they rest), prepare the chimichurri. In a medium bowl, combine the pomegranate seeds, cilantro, parsley, red onion, garlic cloves, and chile, if using. Add the vinegar and lime juice. Stir to combine. Gradually whisk in the olive oil. Season with salt and pepper, to taste.

Let the chimichurri sit at room temperature for at least 15 to 30 minutes to allow the flavors to meld. Stir again just before using.

REST, SLICE, AND SERVE: Once the ribs are tender, remove them from the smoker. If wrapped, carefully unwrap them. Let the ribs rest before slicing. Arrange the ribs on a platter and spoon the fresh, tangy, herb-packed pomegranate chimichurri generously over the top. Serve immediately.

BOSS MOVE

Stir a splash of warm rib jus (from the foil wrap or cutting board) into your chimichurri before serving. It fuses the smoke with the tang and turns that fresh sauce into a flavor nuke.

CHAPTER 6

LAMB, GAME, AND MORE

EXOTIC RIDERS

Welcome to where the wild things sizzle. This next stop is for adventurous eaters and taste explorers. We're talkin' lamb legs, elk, maybe even a little gator if you're feelin' froggy. This is the *Exotic Riders* car, baby. And in here, we ride different. We're using open flames and real smoke to unlock all that wild, gamey soul and turn it into something unforgettable. Whether it's a rack of lamb dressed to kill or smoked boar that eats like a dream, these recipes are built to impress. This section is for when you wanna flex, experiment, or just break out of the same ol' dinner rotation. Time for an adventure.

Covered and Smothered

Rack of Lamb

The very first thing I ever cooked when I got a smoker was a rack of lamb, and it's still one of my all-time favorites. Rich, delicious, and stupid easy to pull off, it's the kind of recipe that makes you look like a pro without breaking a sweat. And honestly, who doesn't love meat on a stick?

SERVES: 2 TO 4

PREP TIME: 15 MINUTES PLUS 30 TO 45 MINUTES REST BEFORE SMOKING

COOK TIME: 1 HOUR 15 MINUTES TO 1 HOUR 30 MINUTES (SMOKE AND SEAR)

REST TIME (AFTER SMOKING AND SEARING): 15 TO 20 MINUTES

LAMB

One 1½-to-2-pound rack of lamb (8-bone), frenched (fat-cap trimmed, bones cleaned)

2 tablespoons extra-virgin olive oil, plus more for the skillet

CHOOSE YOUR RUB

HOMEMADE RUB

1 tablespoon kosher salt

1 tablespoon freshly ground black pepper

1 tablespoon garlic powder

1 tablespoon fresh rosemary leaves, finely chopped

1 teaspoon fresh thyme leaves, finely chopped

PREMADE RUB

2 tablespoons of your favorite high-quality lamb rub or AP BBQ Rub (page 30, or look for one with herbs, garlic, and salt)

FOR SMOKING

Applewood

PREP THE RACK: Pat the rack of lamb dry with paper towels. Drizzle with olive oil and rub to coat. Season the lamb with the rub of your choice. Let the seasoned lamb sit at room temperature for 30 to 45 minutes while you fire up the smoker.

FIRE UP THE SMOKER: Preheat your smoker to 225°F. Add applewood chunks or chips for a subtly sweet smoke that complements the lamb without overpowering it.

SMOKE LOW AND SLOW: Place the rack of lamb bone-side down (fat-cap up) directly on the smoker grates. Smoke until the internal temperature of the thickest part of the meat reaches 115°F to 120°F for medium rare. This will typically take about 1 hour, depending on the size and thickness of the rack. Use a meat thermometer for accuracy.

REST AND HEAT FOR SEAR: Remove the lamb from the smoker and let it rest for about 20 minutes. Meanwhile, get a cast-iron skillet or your grill grates blazing hot (high heat) for searing.

SEAR TO FINISH: Add a touch more oil to the hot skillet if needed (or sear directly on the hot grill grates). Sear each side of the lamb rack, constantly flipping every 30 seconds or so, until a rich crust forms and you've reached your desired temp. Be careful not to overcook. Aim for a final internal temperature of 115˚F to 120˚F. Our finishing sear will bring it to our final temperature.

SLICE AND SERVE: Let the seared rack of lamb rest for another 5 to 10 minutes before slicing. Slice between the bones into individual chops. Serve straight up.

BOSS MOVE

Brush the lamb with melted rosemary-garlic butter right before the final sear. It locks in flavor, boosts the crust, and leaves your guests wondering when you went and got five-star training.

Smoked Braised Lamb

My friends started calling me the "Lamb King" because of this dish, and that's praise I don't take lightly. This smoked braised lamb is one of my most famous plates for a reason. The combo of smoke and braise knocks out any of that gamey flavor, leaving you with meat that's fall-apart tender, juicy, and packed with flavor. Even the folks who swear they don't like lamb end up converted after one bite.

SERVES: 8 TO 10
PREP TIME: 20 MINUTES PLUS 30 TO 45 MINUTES REST BEFORE SMOKING
SMOKE TIME: 3 TO 3½ HOURS
BRAISE TIME: 2 TO 2½ HOURS
REST TIME (AFTER COOKING): 20 TO 30 MINUTES
TOTAL COOK TIME: 5 TO 6 HOURS

LAMB

One 5-to-6-pound boneless lamb shoulder roast, netting removed

2 tablespoons extra-virgin olive oil

CHOOSE YOUR RUB

HOMEMADE RUB

1½ tablespoons kosher salt

1 tablespoon freshly ground black pepper

2 teaspoons garlic powder

2 teaspoons onion powder

1 tablespoon dried oregano

2 teaspoons dried rosemary (crushed if whole leaves)

1 teaspoon smoked paprika

Zest of 1 lemon

PREMADE RUB

2 tablespoons of your favorite lamb rub

FOR SMOKING

Mild fruitwood like apple, oak, or pecan

BRAISING LIQUID

1 large yellow onion, thickly sliced

6 to 8 large cloves garlic, smashed

2 or 3 sprigs fresh rosemary

1½ cups low-sodium beef broth

1 cup dry red wine (such as Cabernet Sauvignon, Syrah, or Merlot)

1 tablespoon soy sauce

PREP AND RUB THE LAMB: If your boneless lamb shoulder has excessive hard fat, trim some of it off, but leave a good layer of fat for flavor and moisture during the long cook. Rub the lamb shoulder all over with olive oil. Generously apply your chosen rub all over the lamb, ensuring even coverage. Let the rubbed lamb sit at room temperature for 30 to 45 minutes while the smoker comes to temperature.

SMOKE THE LAMB: Preheat your smoker to 250°F. Place the lamb directly on the smoker grates (fat-side up, if applicable to your cut). Smoke unwrapped for 3 to 3½ hours, or until a deep, rich bark has formed and the internal temperature of the lamb reaches 160°F to 170°F.

BRAISE THE LAMB: In a large disposable foil pan or a Dutch oven large enough to hold the lamb, create a bed by layering the sliced yellow onion, smashed garlic cloves, and fresh rosemary sprigs. Pour in the beef broth, red wine, and soy sauce.

Carefully transfer the smoked lamb shoulder from the smoker and nestle it into the pan on top of the onions and braising liquid. Cover the pan tightly with heavy-duty aluminum foil (if using a foil pan) or with its lid (if using a Dutch oven).

COOK UNTIL TENDER: Return the covered pan to the smoker (still at 250°F, or you can increase to 275°F to 300°F to speed up the cook slightly, or transfer to a 300°F oven). Continue to cook for another 2 to 2½ hours, or until the lamb is fork-tender and the internal temperature is 200°F to 205°F. The meat should shred easily.

REST, SHRED, AND SERVE: Carefully remove the pan from the smoker or oven. Let the lamb rest in the braising liquid, uncovered (or very loosely tented) for 20 to 30 minutes. Transfer the lamb to a large cutting board or platter. Using two forks or gloved hands, shred the meat, discarding any large pieces of fat or connective tissue.

Optional: Skim the fat from the braising liquid. You can strain the liquid and reduce it slightly on the stovetop to create a more concentrated jus, or simply mix some of the unreduced, flavorful braising liquid into the shredded lamb for extra moisture and richness.

BOSS MOVE

Once the lamb is shredded, hit it with a quick sear in a hot cast-iron skillet with a drizzle of the braising liquid. It crisps up the edges and locks in flavor . . . think lamb carnitas.

Venison Backstrap

Venison backstrap is where my love for wild game kicks in. Cooked right, it's tender, flavorful, and way more approachable than people think. It's the perfect intro to wild game, bold enough to bring that rugged edge but refined enough to impress anyone. With a little care and a lot of flavor, wild game shines every time.

SERVES: 2 TO 4
PREP TIME: 15 MINUTES
COOK TIME: 1 HOUR 20 MINUTES

REVERSE-SEAR (CHOOSE YOUR METHOD)

MARINADE

1 tablespoon extra-virgin olive oil

1 tablespoon Worcestershire sauce

1 teaspoon balsamic vinegar

4 cloves garlic, minced

1 teaspoon chopped fresh rosemary

1 teaspoon freshly ground black pepper

2 teaspoons kosher salt

DRY RUB

1 tablespoon kosher salt

½ tablespoon freshly ground black pepper

1 teaspoon granulated garlic

One 1½-to-2-pound whole venison backstrap, silver skin trimmed

FOR SMOKING

Mild fruitwood like apple or cherry

FINAL SEAR

2 tablespoons unsalted butter

2 tablespoons neutral oil

2 cloves garlic, smashed

2 sprigs fresh rosemary or thyme

SEASON THE VENISON: If marinating, combine all i the marinade ngredients in a small bowl. Whisk together. Coat the venison and marinate for 2 to 3 hours. Pat dry before cooking. If using dry rub, in a small bowl, stir together the rub ingredients and apply to the venison backstrap. Let the rub tack up while you heat your smoker.

HEAT YOUR SMOKER: Preheat your grill or smoker to 225°F for indirect heat.

SMOKE YOUR VENISON: Place the backstrap onto the smoker or your grill over indirect heat. Let it cook slowly until the internal temperature reaches 115°F for rare or 120°F for medium rare. You don't want to overcook venison. Once it reaches your desired temperature, remove the backstrap from the grill and let it rest on a cutting board or wire rack for 10 to 15 minutes.

SEAR IT OFF: While the backstrap rests, crank the heat on a cast-iron skillet. You want it screaming hot for a quick, intense sear. Add the butter, oil, smashed garlic cloves, and fresh rosemary or thyme sprigs to the hot skillet. Once the butter is melted and foaming, carefully place the rested backstrap into the skillet. Sear the backstrap quickly, 30 to 45 seconds per side, continually flipping until a beautiful, dark crust forms. As you sear, continuously baste the meat with the herby butter in the pan using a spoon.

REST AND SERVE: Once seared, remove the backstrap from the skillet and let it rest for another 6 to 8 minutes. This final rest helps lock in the juices. Slice the backstrap across the grain into thick medallions. The center should be a beautiful blushing and juicy pink. Serve immediately.

BOSS MOVE

After searing, hit it with a quick brush of melted beef-tallow butter. Mix the tallow with the butter garlic, parsley, and a squeeze of lemon juice. It'll level out the lean venison and add a beefy punch.

Lavish Lamb Burger

This lamb burger hits every flavor note. It's my tribute to a Bay Area spot that's long gone, but I used to make the trip just for this. Juicy lamb, fresh sprouts, creamy aioli, it all just works. This one keeps those legendary flavors alive.

SERVES: 4

PREP TIME: 15 TO 20 MINUTES

AIOLI CHILL TIME: AT LEAST 15 MINUTES

COOK TIME: 12 TO 15 MINUTES

TOTAL TIME (INCLUDING CHILL TIME): 30 TO 35 MINUTES ACTIVE, 45 MINUTES TOTAL

BLACK GARLIC AIOLI

4 cloves black garlic, mashed into a smooth paste (about 2 tablespoons paste)

½ cup mayonnaise

1 teaspoon freshly squeezed lemon juice

1½ tablespoons Dijon mustard

Kosher salt

LAMB PATTIES

1½ pounds ground lamb

1½ teaspoons kosher salt

1 teaspoon freshly ground black pepper

½ teaspoon smoked paprika

1 teaspoon ground cumin

½ teaspoon garlic powder

1 teaspoon ground sumac

Neutral oil, for the grill (optional)

4 slices sharp white cheddar cheese

BURGER BUILD

Unsalted butter, for toasting

4 brioche or potato buns

1 cup crunchy sprouts (such as alfalfa or broccoli sprouts)

Thinly sliced red onion (optional)

Tomato slices (optional)

MAKE THE BLACK GARLIC AIOLI: In a small bowl, combine the black garlic paste, mayonnaise, lemon juice, and Dijon mustard. Stir well until completely smooth. Season with salt to taste. Cover and refrigerate for at least 15 minutes to allow the flavors to meld. This can be made a day ahead.

FORM THE LAMB PATTIES: Form your ground lamb into nice, thick, steak house–style patties. Press a small dimple in the center with your thumb to help them cook evenly. In a small bowl, mix together the salt, pepper, paprika, cumin, garlic powder, and sumac. Season the patties generously.

COOK THE PATTIES: Preheat your grill or a griddle or cast-iron skillet over medium-high heat. Lightly oil the grill grates or skillet if needed. Cook the lamb patties for 4 to 5 minutes per side for medium (internal temperature of 145°F), or to your desired doneness. During the last minute of cooking, place a slice of cheese on top of each patty and cover (with a lid or a heatproof bowl) to melt the cheese.

TOAST THE BUNS: Lightly butter the cut sides of the buns. Toast them cut-side down on the grill, griddle, or in a pan until golden brown and crisp.

ASSEMBLE THE BURGERS: Spread a generous layer of black garlic aioli on the cut side of the bottom bun. Lay down a proper pile of sprouts. Place the cheddar-topped lamb patty on top. Add red onion and tomato slices, if using. Spread more aioli on the cut side of the top bun. Place the top bun on the burger and serve immediately, while hot.

FLAVOR BOOST: Baste the patties with rosemary butter in the last minute of searing. Melt the butter with a smashed garlic clove and rosemary, then spoon it over. It adds that rich, herby flavor that takes the lamb to the next level without losing its edge.

Thai Grilled Quail

I still remember my first grilled quail at a Bay Area Vietnamese spot called Ben Tre . . . I was hooked instantly. Crazy juicy, loaded with flavor, and had me driving across the bay just to get my fix. Finally said forget it and made my own. This version brings all that same fire, straight off your grill.

SERVES: 4 SERVINGS
PREP TIME: 15 MINUTES
MARINATE TIME: 2 TO 4 HOURS
COOK TIME: 10 TO 12 MINUTES
TOTAL TIME (EXCLUDING MARINATING): 25 TO 30 MINUTES

QUAIL AND MARINADE

8 whole quails

4 cloves garlic, minced

1 tablespoon grated fresh ginger

3 tablespoons fish sauce

1 tablespoon soy sauce

1 tablespoon brown sugar

1 tablespoon freshly squeezed lime juice

1 teaspoon lime zest (optional, but adds brightness)

1 tablespoon neutral oil (such as canola or avocado)

½ teaspoon freshly ground black pepper

1 small Thai chile, finely chopped (optional, for a kick; adjust to heat preference)

DIPPING SAUCE (OPTIONAL)

2 tablespoons fish sauce

2 tablespoons freshly squeezed lime juice

1 teaspoon granulated sugar, plus more as needed

1 small clove garlic, minced

1 Thai chile, thinly sliced (optional)

PREPARE AND MARINATE THE QUAIL: To spatchcock the quail: Place the quail breast-side down. Using sturdy kitchen shears, cut along both sides of the backbone to remove it. Flip the quail over and press down firmly on the breastbone to flatten it.

In a medium bowl or a large zip-top bag, combine the garlic cloves, ginger, fish sauce, soy sauce, brown sugar, lime juice, lime zest, if using, neutral oil, pepper, and the chile, if using. Add the prepared quail to the marinade and toss or turn to coat them evenly. Cover the bowl or seal the bag and marinate in the refrigerator for at least 2 hours but no more than 4 hours; quail are small and absorb flavor quickly.

PREHEAT THE GRILL: Preheat your grill to medium-high heat (375°F to 400°F). Clean the grill grates thoroughly and oil them well to prevent the quail from sticking.

GRILL THE QUAIL: Remove the quail from the marinade, allowing any excess marinade to drip off (do not pat them completely dry, as some marinade on the surface helps with caramelization). Discard the leftover marinade. Place the quail on the hot, oiled grill grates, skin-side down.

Grill for 4 to 6 minutes per side, or until beautifully charred, the skin is crispy, and the internal temperature in the thickest part (thigh) reaches 160°F to 165°F. Because they are small, quail cook quickly, so watch them carefully to avoid overcooking. If flare-ups occur, move the quail to a cooler part of the grill temporarily.

REST AND SERVE: Remove the grilled quail from the grill and let them rest on a cutting board, loosely tented with foil, for about 5 minutes before serving. Serve hot. They are traditionally eaten with your hands. Offer extra lime wedges for squeezing and fresh herbs like cilantro or Thai basil on the side.

PREPARE OPTIONAL DIPPING SAUCE (NUOC CHAM): If making the dipping sauce: In a small bowl, whisk together the fish sauce, lime juice, 1 tablespoon water, granulated sugar to taste, garlic clove, and chile, if using. Stir until the sugar is completely dissolved. Taste and adjust the balance of sweet, salty, sour, and spicy to your preference. Serve alongside the grilled quail.

BOSS MOVE

Brush the quail with a little dipping sauce near the end so it caramelizes on the skin. Finish with a squeeze of lime juice and a sprinkle of crispy shallots or toasted rice powder. Flavor packin' for real!

Lamb Chops with Mint Chimi

Lamb chops are like little mini T-bones, and I can never get enough of them. And nothing hits harder with lamb than mint. That's why I whipped up this mint chimichurri! It's fresh, zesty, and so good you'll be spooning it on everything once you try it. Trust me, this one's about to be your new obsession.

SERVES: 4

PREP TIME: 15 MINUTES PLUS 30 MINUTES MARINATING, OR UP TO 4 HOURS

COOK TIME: 8 TO 10 MINUTES

REST TIME: 5 MINUTES

LAMB CHOPS

2 tablespoons extra-virgin olive oil

1 tablespoon minced garlic

1 tablespoon finely chopped fresh rosemary leaves

1 tablespoon finely chopped fresh thyme leaves

1 teaspoon lemon zest

1½ teaspoons kosher salt

1 teaspoon freshly ground black pepper

8 lamb rib chops (each 1 to 1½ inches thick)

MINT-CILANTRO CHIMICHURRI

½ cup finely chopped fresh mint leaves

½ cup finely chopped fresh cilantro leaves and tender stems

½ cup finely chopped fresh flat-leaf parsley

1 tablespoon finely chopped fresh oregano or 1½ teaspoon dried oregano

3 cloves garlic, finely minced

½ teaspoon red pepper flakes (optional, for heat)

Zest of 1 lemon

2 tablespoons champagne vinegar or red wine vinegar

½ cup extra-virgin olive oil

Kosher salt and freshly ground black pepper

MARINATE THE LAMB CHOPS: In a small bowl, mix together the olive oil, garlic, rosemary, thyme, lemon zest, salt, and black pepper. Rub this mixture all over the lamb chops, ensuring they are evenly coated.

Let the chops sit at room temperature for at least 30 minutes before grilling. Alternatively, you can cover and refrigerate them for up to 4 hours; if refrigerated, bring them to room temperature for 20 to 30 minutes before grilling.

MAKE THE MINT-CILANTRO CHIMICHURRI (WHILE THE LAMB MARINATES OR RESTS): In a medium bowl, combine the mint, cilantro, parsley, oregano, garlic cloves, red pepper flakes, if using, and the lemon zest. Stir in the vinegar.

Gradually whisk in the olive oil until well combined. Season with salt and black pepper to taste. For best flavor, let the chimichurri sit at room temperature for at least 15 minutes (or up to a few hours) to allow the flavors to meld. Stir again before serving.

GRILL THE LAMB CHOPS: Preheat your grill to medium-high heat (400°F to 450°F). Clean and oil the grill grates. Place the marinated lamb chops on the hot grill. Grill for 3 to 4 minutes per side for medium rare (internal temperature of 130°F to 135°F), or adjust the cooking time for your preferred doneness. For medium, aim for 135°F to 140°F. Remove the lamb chops from the grill and let them rest on a cutting board, loosely tented with foil, for 5 minutes before serving.

SERVE: Arrange the rested lamb chops on a platter or individual plates. Top each chop generously with a spoonful of the fresh mint-cilantro chimichurri.

FLAVOR BOOST: Chop up a few oil-cured olives and fold them into the chimichurri right before serving. That briny, salty punch levels up the freshness and adds a rich umami contrast that elevates every bite.

Black Magic Lamb Ribs

These are my ode to how much I love cooking with lamb. Tender, rich, and perfect for BBQ. And that Black Magic glaze? So damn good you'll want to drink it by the gallon. Put the two together and you've got a rack that's guaranteed to steal the show.

SERVES: 3 TO 4
PREP TIME: 15 MINUTES
COOK TIME: ABOUT 3 HOURS

WOOD

Hickory, oak, or pecan

LAMB RIBS

2 racks lamb ribs (Denver style or riblets, 2 to 2½ pounds total)

2 tablespoons neutral oil (such as canola or vegetable)

RUB

2 tablespoons kosher salt

1 tablespoon freshly ground black pepper

1 tablespoon smoked paprika

1 teaspoon garlic powder

1 teaspoon onion powder

½ teaspoon ground cumin (optional)

UPGRADED KENTUCKY BLACK SAUCE

¾ cup Worcestershire sauce

¼ cup white vinegar

¼ cup apple cider vinegar

2 tablespoons soy sauce

2 tablespoons water

2 tablespoons brown sugar

1 tablespoon freshly squeezed lemon juice

1 tablespoon Dijon mustard

½ tablespoon freshly ground black pepper

1 teaspoon kosher salt

½ teaspoon smoked paprika

2 large cloves garlic, grated or minced

1 tablespoon unsalted butter

PREP THE LAMB RIBS: If present, remove the silver skin (thin membrane) from the bone side of the lamb ribs using a paper towel for grip. This helps the rub penetrate and makes the ribs more tender. Rub the ribs all over with neutral oil.

In a small bowl, mix together the salt, pepper, smoked paprika, garlic powder, onion powder, and cumin, if using. Season the lamb ribs generously on all sides with this rub mixture. Let the seasoned ribs sit at room temperature while the smoker preheats.

FIRE UP THE SMOKER: Preheat your smoker to 250°F. Use a bold wood like hickory, oak, or pecan, which pairs well with lamb.

SMOKE THE RIBS (INITIAL SMOKE): Place the ribs bone-side down directly on the smoker grates. Smoke at 250°F for 2 to 2½ hours, or until a rich, dark bark has formed and the meat has started to pull back slightly from the ends of the bones.

MAKE THE UPGRADED KENTUCKY BLACK SAUCE: While the ribs are smoking (or about an hour before you plan to baste), prepare the sauce. In a small saucepan, combine all the sauce ingredients *except* the butter. Bring the mixture to a simmer over medium-low heat. Cook, stirring occasionally, for 10 to 12 minutes to allow the flavors to meld and the sauce to reduce slightly.

Turn off the heat and whisk in the butter until melted, and the sauce is smooth and glossy. Keep the sauce warm for basting.

BASTE AND FINISH SMOKING: During the last 30 to 45 minutes of the smoking process, begin basting the lamb ribs with the warm Kentucky black sauce. Apply a light coat every 10 to 15 minutes. Continue smoking until the ribs are tender and juicy, with an internal temperature of 195°F to 200°F. The meat should be very tender but not necessarily "fall off the bone" like pork ribs; lamb ribs have a slightly different texture.

REST AND SERVE: Remove the ribs from the smoker and let them rest, tented loosely with foil, for about 10 minutes before slicing. Slice between the bones. Drizzle with a little more of the warm black sauce before serving.

BOSS MOVE

After the final baste, crank the heat to 300°F for 10 minutes to let that black sauce turn into a sticky, caramelized glaze. Finish with chopped rosemary and lemon zest before serving. Fireworks!

Elk with Blueberry Sauce

This dish turns heads. Rich, wild elk meets a sweet, tangy blueberry sauce that feels fancy but totally approachable. It's easy to make, looks award-worthy, and proves bold flavors can be simple, beautiful, and unforgettable.

SERVES: 2 TO 3

PREP TIME: 15 MINUTES PLUS 30 MINUTES REST BEFORE SMOKING

SMOKE TIME: 45 MINUTES TO 1 HOUR

SAUCE COOK TIME: 10 TO 15 MINUTES

SEAR TIME: 2 TO 4 MINUTES

REST TIME (AFTER SEARING): 10 MINUTES

TOTAL TIME (EXCLUDING REST): 1 HOUR TO 1 HOUR 20 MINUTES

ELK BACKSTRAP

1½ to 2 pounds elk backstrap (loin), trimmed well of silver skin

1 tablespoon extra-virgin olive oil

1½ teaspoons kosher salt

1 teaspoon freshly ground black pepper

1 teaspoon garlic powder

½ teaspoon dried thyme or 1 teaspoon finely chopped fresh thyme leaves

½ teaspoon crushed juniper berries (optional, for a wild-forest vibe)

Neutral oil (such as grapeseed or avocado), for searing

FOR SMOKING

Mild fruitwood like cherry or apple

HERBACEOUS BLUEBERRY-WINE SAUCE

2 tablespoons cold unsalted butter, divided

1 small shallot, finely minced

1 clove garlic, finely minced

1 cup fresh or frozen (no need to thaw) blueberries

¾ cup dry red wine

1 tablespoon balsamic vinegar

1 tablespoon honey or maple syrup

1 tablespoon finely chopped fresh rosemary, thyme, or tarragon

Pinch of kosher salt

PREP THE ELK BACKSTRAP: Pat the elk backstrap dry with paper towels. Rub it all over with the olive oil. In a small bowl, combine the salt, pepper, garlic powder, thyme, and juniper berries, if using. Season the elk backstrap evenly on all sides with this rub mixture. Let the seasoned backstrap sit at room temperature for about 30 minutes while you preheat the smoker.

SMOKE THE ELK: Preheat your smoker to 225°F. Place the elk backstrap directly on the smoker grates. Smoke until the internal temperature of the thickest part reaches 115°F to 120°F for medium rare. This usually takes 45 minutes to 1 hour, depending on the thickness of the backstrap. Use a reliable meat thermometer.

MAKE THE WINE SAUCE: In a saucepan over medium heat, melt 1 tablespoon of the butter. Add the shallot and garlic; cook 2 to 3 minutes until soft and fragrant. Stir in the blueberries, red wine, balsamic vinegar, honey or maple syrup, rosemary, and salt. Simmer for 10 to 15 minutes, lightly mash some berries, and reduce until slightly thick. Remove from the heat and whisk in the remaining 1 tablespoon butter until smooth and glossy. Keep warm.

SEAR IT HOT (REVERSE SEAR): Once the elk reaches 115°F to 120°F in the smoker, remove it. Get a cast-iron skillet screaming hot over high heat. Add a drizzle of neutral oil to the pan. Carefully place the smoked elk backstrap in the hot skillet. Sear for 1 to 2 minutes per side, until a deep, rich crust forms all around. Aim for a final internal temperature of 125°F to 130°F for medium rare.

REST AND SERVE: Transfer the seared elk backstrap to a cutting board. Tent loosely with foil and let it rest for 10 minutes before slicing. This allows the juices to redistribute. Slice the elk backstrap against the grain into medallions about ½ inch thick. Arrange the medallions on plates and spoon the warm herbaceous blueberry-wine sauce generously over the top. Garnish with a sprig of fresh rosemary or thyme for a touch of woodland elegance, if desired.

FLAVOR BOOST: After slicing, hit those elk medallions with Maldon salt and a little orange zest. That citrus lift makes the blueberry pop and gives the whole dish that top-chef vibe.

Gator Tots

These ain't your average nuggets. These are gator tots, and they bite back. Juicy alligator chunks soaked in buttermilk and hot sauce, fried golden with that Cajun crunch that hits like a snare drum. Most folks will think they're chicken nuggets till that flavor hits. The perfect intro to exotic eats, and once you dunk 'em in that tangy Worcestershire aioli, it's game over.

SERVES: 4 TO 6 AS AN APPETIZER

PREP TIME: 20 MINUTES

MARINATE TIME: AT LEAST 30 MINUTES AND UP TO 4 HOURS (OPTIONAL, BUT RECOMMENDED)

COOK TIME: 8 TO 10 MINUTES (FRYING IN BATCHES)

TANGY WORCESTERSHIRE AIOLI

½ cup mayonnaise

1 tablespoon Worcestershire sauce

1 tablespoon freshly squeezed lemon juice

1 teaspoon Dijon mustard

1 clove garlic, finely grated or minced

½ teaspoon hot sauce, plus more as needed

Pinch of smoked paprika

Kosher salt and freshly ground black pepper

GATOR TOTS AND MARINADE

1½ pounds alligator meat (tenderloin or tail meat recommended), cut into bite-size nuggets (1-to-1½ inch pieces)

1 cup buttermilk

1 tablespoon hot sauce (such as Bear & Burton's Special Reserve)

½ tablespoon garlic powder

½ tablespoon onion powder

½ teaspoon paprika (sweet or smoked)

½ teaspoon kosher salt

¼ teaspoon freshly ground black pepper

BREADING

1 cup all-purpose flour

½ cup yellow cornmeal (fine or medium grind)

1 tablespoon Cajun seasoning or your favorite all-purpose spice blend with a kick

½ teaspoon baking powder (for extra crispiness)

FOR FRYING

Neutral oil (peanut, canola, or vegetable)

Kosher salt

MAKE THE TANGY WORCESTERSHIRE AIOLI: In a small bowl, whisk together the mayonnaise, Worcestershire sauce, lemon juice, mustard, garlic, hot sauce, and smoked paprika until completely smooth. Season with salt and pepper to taste. Cover and refrigerate until ready to use, allowing the flavors to meld (at least 15 to 20 minutes is good).

MARINATE THE ALLIGATOR (OPTIONAL BUT RECOMMENDED; 30 MINUTES TO 4 HOURS): In a medium bowl, whisk together the buttermilk, hot sauce, garlic powder, onion powder, paprika, salt, and pepper. Add the 1½ pounds of alligator nuggets to the buttermilk mixture, ensuring they are well coated. Cover the bowl and refrigerate for at least 30 minutes, or up to 4 hours, to tenderize and flavor the meat.

MAKE THE BREADING: In a large bowl, combine all the ingredients for the breading.

BREAD THE ALLIGATOR NUGGETS: Remove the alligator nuggets from the buttermilk marinade, allowing any excess marinade to drip off. Working with a few pieces at a time, toss the nuggets in the seasoned flour mixture until they are thoroughly and evenly coated. Press gently to ensure the breading adheres well. Place the breaded nuggets on a wire rack or a clean plate as you work.

FRY THE GATOR TOTS: Heat 1 to 1½ inches of neutral oil in a large, heavy-bottomed skillet or Dutch oven (or use a deep fryer) over medium heat to 350°F to 365°F. Use a thermometer to monitor the oil temperature. Once the oil is hot, carefully add the breaded alligator nuggets in a single layer, being sure not to overcrowd the pan; fry in batches if necessary.

Fry for 2 to 3 minutes per side, or until the nuggets are golden brown, crispy, and cooked through (alligator meat cooks quickly and can become tough if overcooked). Remove the fried gator tots with a slotted spoon or spider and transfer them to a paper towel-lined plate or a wire rack to drain. Sprinkle lightly with salt while they are still hot.

SERVE: Serve hot with a generous side of the prepared tangy Worcestershire aioli for dipping.

BOSS MOVE

Take these gator tots straight into po' boy territory. Use my Shrimp Not So Po' Boy recipe (page 126), replace the shrimp with the tots, and enjoy.

CHAPTER 7

COCKTAILS

THE LOUNGE CAR

Drinks aren't just something to sip while waiting on ribs. They're part of the ***performance***. A well-made cocktail sets the tone. It cools the heat, sharpens the vibe, and makes everything taste a little better. Just like your food, your drinks should be bold, balanced, and built with intention. This section's not about fussy mixology or twelve-ingredient experiments. It's about flavor, flow, and punch-you-in-the-chest personality. Whether you're handing someone a chilled sidecar or a smoky espresso martini, you're not just serving a drink. You're pouring a moment. A vibe. A flavor signature. These cocktails hit hard, sip smooth, and remind everyone who's running the party.

Hit Hard,
Sip Smooth

RAW

Chuck's Sidecar

YIELD: 1 COCKTAIL

2 ounces cognac (go with something solid, nothing dusty)

¾ ounce orange liqueur (Cointreau or Grand Marnier—pick your fighter)

¾ ounce freshly squeezed lemon juice

Sugar, for the rim, if you're feeling sweet

Lemon twist, for garnish (optional)

This is for the bosses, top hats, OGs, and macks.

HOW TO MAKE IT: Fill a shaker with ice, pour in all the ingredients (except the sugar and lemon twist), and shake like you're waking up late for work. Strain the mix into a coupe glass. If you rimmed the glass with sugar, cool. If not, also cool. Garnish with a lemon twist if you like or just raise your glass and let the drink speak for itself. This one doesn't whisper—it sings like a brass band in velvet.

French Connection

YIELD: 1 COCKTAIL

1½ ounces cognac

1½ ounces amaretto

Easy AF, but fancy like Nancy.

HOW TO MAKE IT: Pour the cognac and amaretto over a big ol' ice cube into a rocks glass. Stir it slow—this one doesn't need bells or whistles. It's sweet, it's rich, it goes down like a love song with a bite. Hand this to someone and they'll think you've got stock in silk sheets and slow jams.

Ranch Water, Flavor Train Style

YIELD: 1 COCKTAIL

Juice of 1 lime

2 ounces blanco tequila (I like Santo)

4 to 6 ounces sparkling water (Topo Chico is my fave . . . but use yours)

Pinch of flaky salt

Grilled lime wheel, for garnish (optional)

Drink this in the daylight if you wanna make it to the night.

HOW TO MAKE IT: Fill a tall glass with ice. Squeeze in that lime juice, pour in your tequila, and top it with Topo Chico or the sparkling water of your choice. Give it a lazy stir and hit it with a pinch of salt on top. Garnish with a grilled lime wheel if you're feelin' fancy. It's light, crisp, and sneaky strong. Tastes like sunshine and good decisions.

Smoked Espresso Martini

YIELD: 1 COCKTAIL

Smoked salt, for the rim (optional, but killer)

½ ounce vodka

1 ounce cold-brew concentrate or a strong shot of espresso

¾ ounce coffee liqueur (Kahlúa, Mr. Black, whatever hits)

Dash of chocolate bitters (optional, but it slaps)

3 coffee beans to flex

When the "–itis" sets in, this will get you right.

HOW TO MAKE IT: Rim your glass with a little smoked salt if you want that BBQ barista vibe. Fill your shaker with ice, toss in the vodka, coffee, liqueur, and bitters, if using. Shake the hell out of it—this drink needs a frothy top like a fresh Guinness. Strain into a coupe glass, garnish with three beans like you know the code, and sip like it's two a.m. and the night owes you something.

The Afterburner

Welcome to the after-party! This is what every pitmaster is truly looking forward to. You fired up the grill, laid down some serious smoke, and showed the whole block what hospitality really feels like. But let's be honest: If you're gonna cook like a legend, you might as well party like one too. Because here's the thing. Great BBQ doesn't end when the meat hits the board. It's not just about feeding people. It's about feeding *moments* and celebrating life. The drinks, the music, the vibe . . . they're the secret sauce that makes your food unforgettable. It's what turns a backyard dinner into a memory. What turns good company into lifelong stories. The food is the fire starter, but the party is the blaze. This part of the Flavor Train is where the smoke fades and the spotlight shifts. You pass the tongs, pour a round, and crank the volume just a little louder. It's where the cook takes a breath, steps out from behind the pit, and becomes the host. The vibe-setter. The one who turns "thanks for the food" into "we're never forgetting tonight." So, here it is. Your permission slip to celebrate. Loudly. Fully. Authentically. These are your go-to party tricks and your no-skip playlists. The tools for throwing a bash that matches the flavor you just dropped on their plates. Because you didn't just serve a meal. You built an experience. Welcome to the afterburner.

Don't get it twisted, when you're the one running the pit, *you're* the main event. But once the meat's rested and the plates start flying, it's time to level up the experience. This is where you pull out all the stops. The party tricks. The crowd-pleasers. The jaw-dropping, camera-ready moments that make folks say, "What *is* this man on?" These aren't just gimmicks. These are finishing moves. The sizzle after the sear. The little details that make your cookout feel like a catered concert with smoke instead of spotlights. Bring the fun, bring the flair, and don't be afraid to show off a little.

TRULY
BUD LIGHT
LAGUNITAS

ENTERTAINING YOUR TRAVELERS

Look. Life's not about being perfect. It's about being *present*. Whether you're slinging steaks for two or throwing a backyard rager for twenty-five, don't overthink it. Have fun. Be loud. Be weird. Be *you*. Try new things. Burn something once in a while. Laugh when the sauce explodes. And keep chasing that feeling . . . that moment when a group of people you love takes a bite, looks up, and says, "Damn, this is good!" That's the stuff. That's why we cook. That's why we gather. So, get out there. Fire it up. Turn the music up a little louder. Pour a drink, crack a joke, and chase your flavor dream like it owes you money. The Flavor Train doesn't run on perfection. It runs on passion. And, trust me, you've got it in spades.

The Barbecuterie Board

Put out a giant board stacked with sliced brisket, pork belly, ribs, sausage links, and grilled veggies. Garnish it with charred lemons, herbs, and little ramekins of sauce and pickles. Walk out like you're holding the Olympic torch. Everyone will follow you.

Sauce Station

Set up a sauce bar with whiskey glasses full of dipping sauces. Think Alabama White Sauce (page 35), chipotle peach, Sweet and Smoky BBQ Sauce (page 34), spicy vinegar. Let people dunk wings, rib tips, and grilled shrimp. It's fun, messy, and deeply personal. Like therapy, but saucier.

Party Ice Bath 2.0

Fill a cooler with water, ice, and a handful of kosher salt. It'll chill your beers in under 10 minutes. Bonus move: Toss in a few glow sticks or citrus peels for party esthetics.

Grilled Garnishes Galore

Throw limes, lemons, pineapples, and jalapeños on the grill. Use them in cocktails, as plate garnishes, or just to stunt. Adds smoke, color, and instant "Whoa, who did this?" energy.

Brisket Breakfast Sandwich Bar

Next day? Slice leftover brisket thin, warm it in a skillet, and set out a build-your-own breakfast sandwich station with English muffins, eggs, cheese, and hot sauce. You didn't just host a party. You created a lifestyle.

Flavor Train Radio

Look, good food hits harder when the music's right. You ever reverse sear a ribeye to "Regulate" or slice a brisket while "Dreams" by Fleetwood Mac is playing? That's what we call a "vibe"! This section is all about setting the tone. Backyard BBQs, solo grill sessions, pregame hangs, late-night bites, I got a playlist for all of it. Whether you're in a two-step mood or you're trying to rap along while your tongs are in the air, I got you. From Bay Area slaps to classic rock, disco grooves to guilty pleasure bangers, these are the tracks that have been riding shotgun on the Flavor Train. So, throw on a playlist, crack a cold one, and let the music do what it does best.

Official Like a Ref with a Whistle!

Barbecue Rap (Bay Area Slaps)

1. Mac Dre, "Feelin' Myself"
2. E-40, "Tell Me When to Go"
3. Andre Nickatina, "Ayo for Yayo"
4. P-Lo, "Put Me on Somethin'"
5. Keak da Sneak, "Super Hyphy"
6. The Jacka, "Glamorous Lifestyle"
7. SOB x RBE, "Anti"
8. Nef the Pharaoh, "Big Tymin"
9. Too $hort, "Blow the Whistle"
10. Mistah F.A.B., "N.E.W. Oakland"
11. Larry June, "Smoothies in 1991"
12. Saweetie, "Tap In"
13. G-Eazy, "Calm Down"
14. IAMSU!, "Hella Good"
15. Clyde Carson, "Slow Down"

Classic Rock for the Backyard

1. The Allman Brothers Band, "Ramblin' Man"
2. Creedence Clearwater Revival, "Born on the Bayou"
3. Bob Seger, "Night Moves"
4. The Doobie Brothers, "Long Train Runnin'"
5. Tom Petty and the Heartbreakers, "Mary Jane's Last Dance"
6. Steve Miller Band, "Take The Money And Run"
7. ZZ Top, "Tush"
8. Lynyrd Skynyrd, "Tuesday's Gone"
9. Fleetwood Mac, "Go Your Own Way"
10. The Rolling Stones, "Beast of Burden"
11. Led Zeppelin, "Fool in the Rain"
12. Eagles, "Take It Easy"
13. Bad Company, "Feel Like Makin' Love"
14. Boston, "More Than a Feeling"
15. Eric Clapton, "Cocaine"

Disco and Feel-Good Grooves

1. Earth, Wind & Fire, "September"
2. Bee Gees, "You Should Be Dancing"
3. CHIC, "Le Freak"
4. Donna Summer, "Bad Girls"
5. KC and the Sunshine Band, "Boogie Shoes"
6. Diana Ross, "I'm Coming Out"
7. Rick James, "Super Freak"
8. Gloria Gaynor, "I Will Survive"
9. The Trammps, "Disco Inferno"
10. The Pointer Sisters, "I'm So Excited"
11. Sylvester, "You Make Me Feel (Mighty Real)"
12. Patrice Rushen, "Forget Me Nots"
13. Michael Jackson, "Don't Stop 'til You Get Enough"
14. Prince, "I Wanna Be Your Lover"
15. Heatwave, "Boogie Nights"

Nineties Rock and Pop Nostalgia

1. Sublime, "Santeria"
2. Third Eye Blind, "Semi-Charmed Life"
3. No Doubt, "Just a Girl"
4. TLC, "No Scrubs"
5. OutKast, "Ms. Jackson"
6. Montell Jordan, "This Is How We Do It"
7. Alanis Morissette, "You Learn"
8. Smash Mouth, "Walkin' on the Sun"
9. Counting Crows, "Mr. Jones"
10. Salt-N-Pepa, "Shoop"
11. Gin Blossoms, "Hey Jealousy"
12. Matchbox Twenty, "3AM"
13. Destiny's Child, "Say My Name"
14. Mariah Carey, "Fantasy"
15. Will Smith, "Gettin' Jiggy Wit It"

Thank You

Holy shit. We did it. We made a cookbook. And I say *we* because none of this would've been possible without *you*. If you ever watched a video of mine, tried my food, hired me for a gig, or if you're reading this now, then you helped make this happen. I call it the "flavorgang" for a reason. It's not just a name, it's a crew. A family. Teamwork makes the dream work, and, damn, we really did it. I never dreamed about doing this, but I'm so damn glad I did.

To everyone who's followed me on this wild ride, whether you've been down since the early days or just hopped on the train recently, thank you. Every single view, comment, share, save, like, repost, dupe, stitch, DM, text, or tag . . . it all counts. TikTok, Instagram, YouTube, Facebook, Threads, Pinterest, all of it. You've let me into your homes, your kitchens, and your lives. You've tagged me in family dinners, tailgates, and weeknight wins. You've hyped me up when I was on fire and held it down when I needed it. I never take that for granted. I say "we" because it's always been us. This cookbook? It's as much yours as it is mine.

To the BBQ fam, the ones who live this life and know what it means to bleed hickory, sweat liquor, and hustle with heart. Whether we met at a cook-off or in the comments, you've shown me what community really is. I'll never forget the early follows like BigJohnsBBQ, GroarkBoysBBQ, GrillinWithDad, and CanuckSmoker. Or early reposts like when Kurt from Caribeque posted my pork butt. That shit felt like I had made the cover of *People* magazine. Y'all are the real deal. It's not about numbers. It's about showing up, putting out love, and lifting others up along the way. And that's what all ya'll have done for me. If you ever shared a post, dropped a comment, hit me with a "bro, this slapped," or just silently supported, I see you, and I appreciate you.

To my *Borrachos Cocinos*, my brothers. Eric, Anthony, AJ. The crew. My early morning beer boys. We didn't win any major championships, unless "most liquor consumed during a day" counts. But we built something better. We bonded through fire, smoke, long-ass days, and a whole lot of beer. We fed people. We brought joy. We made money and memories. And we're just getting started. I love you fools like brothers. *BORRACHOS COCINOS* forever.

To my NorCal and Bay Area BBQ folks: Look what y'all did. I remember hearing "there's no such thing as California BBQ" or "Bay BBQ doesn't exist." And I remember how wrong they were. From brick-and-mortar joints to backyard pop-ups, to millions and millions of followers and hundreds of millions of views, we put the Bay on the map. From winning People's Choice in Key West to placing at the Texas Open Fire Meat Up. From TFTI's birthday bashes to stepping onto major stages like Memphis in May and SmokeSlam. Tone, Nick W, Nick K, Pete, Kevin, Corey, Dan, Rob . . . I ride with y'all forever.

To my friends . . . the ones that I've known my whole life . . . the ones who've held me down through the chaos. The ones who stuck around even when I disappeared into deadlines or got lost in my own head. I know I'm not the best at texting back. I go quiet. But y'all never gave up on me. You didn't just stand by me. You reminded me who I was. Matt, Ryan, Bryan, Joe, Danny, Bryce, Nic . . . thank you. You're the kind of men I look up to. You've had my back through it all. Just, thank you.

To my family . . . boy, oh, boy. Despite being known as the fun-loving little brother, the ridiculous uncle, the lovable screw-up . . . I hope you know how much I love you and how hard I try every day to make you proud. Being adopted into this family was the greatest gift I've ever received. You gave me love, laughter, second chances, and a sense of purpose I didn't even know I was missing. I had the coolest big brother. The most loving big sisters. A little sister, Zee, who keeps me guessing and grounded. A nephew who was my best friend. Two nieces I'd do anything for. My life is incredible. Like, actually the kind of life people write books and movies about. And that's not just because of Mom and Dad. It's because of all of you.

Speaking of Dad. Pop, you are *the* dad. When I think about what it means to be a good man, a good husband, a good father, I see you. You fell in love with Mom, started a family young, and made it work. Not everyone does that. You supported everyone, and you always let Mom shine. And when life gave you the chance to do it all over again, you said "Yes." You and Mom changed my life. Forever. You changed Zee's life. Forever.

I don't know if you ever missed a single little league game. The one time Mom had to leave early, I remember you calling her from the car just to say, "You just missed it . . . Chucker hit a walk-off home run." You were at every football game in high school. Heat, rain, wind—you were there. Pacing the sideline like a defensive coordinator. I remember the notes you'd leave me in the mornings during recruiting season. I remember the folder you kept with clippings and photos. You're the reason I love minestrone, cioppino, and clam chowder. You're the reason I know a proper steak is medium rare at most. And that an overcooked prime rib can ruin Christmas dinner. You took me to Giants games, 49ers games, Bodega Bay, Lake Tahoe . . . you made everything feel like a moment. You made life feel special.

I know I wasn't always easy. I know I stressed you out. When you found lighters and I said they were for "fireworks" or claimed my shirt smelled like smoke because of a "campfire," I'm sure you knew I was lying. I made some bad choices. But I always wanted to make you proud. That was always the goal. Even when I didn't say it. And, now, as a grown man and a dad myself, I know you're proud. You sent me a text out of nowhere telling me how proud you are of the family I'm raising. And, Pop, that right there . . . that's all I've ever wanted.

Erica. My wife. My partner. My everything. None of this happens without you. You've held it down through the crazy schedules, the deadlines, the long cooks, the last-minute shoots. You've supported me when I was on top of the world and loved me just as hard when I wasn't. You've made our home feel like peace. You've shown me what love looks like when it's tested and still stands strong. I'm a better man because of you. I'm a better dad because of you. You're the backbone of this whole thing, even when you're not in front of the camera. Thank you for believing in me when I didn't.

And to my daughter, Amaya. You are my light. You are joy and magic and fire and everything good in this world. You make me want to be great. When you grow up and read this, I hope you know your dad chased his dreams. I hope you know that everything he built, he built with you in mind. Every recipe, every story, every moment of this book has your fingerprints on it. I hope you see what's possible when you move with love, with purpose, and with heart. I hope you know I did this for you.

I love you both with everything I've got.

To all ya'll, thank you for my life.

Your son, brother, uncle, friend, husband, and dad,

CHUCK

BANG BANG FLAVORGANG!

Index

D

E

F

G

S

About the Author

Chuck Matto is the founder of Chuck's Flavor Train, a BBQ-driven brand built on making great food approachable, fun, and never intimidating. His cooking journey began in the backyard, where weekend cookouts for friends slowly turned into a lifelong pursuit of smoke, fire, and big, bold flavor. That backyard spirit still guides everything he does today, whether he is feeding a crowd, testing a new idea, or throwing something on the pit simply because it sounded good.

Chuck has competed on Food Network's *BBQ Brawl* and Cooking Channel's *Fire Masters,* and has earned BBQ awards from coast to coast. Through social media, catering, live demonstrations, private classes, and hands-on teaching, he shares his love of BBQ with audiences near and far. If it involves food and bringing people together, chances are he is already loading the cooler and grabbing the tongs.

Chuck Matto
WATCH ME ON FOOD NETWORK
INSTAGRAM: @chucksflavortrain
TIKTOK: @chucksflavortrain
#bangbangflavorgang

weldon**owen**
an imprint of Insight Editions
P.O. Box 3088
San Rafael, CA 94912
www.weldonowen.com

CEO Raoul Goff
SVP Group Publisher Jeff McLaughlin
VP Publisher Roger Shaw
Executive Editor Edward Ash-Milby
Assistant Editor Kayla Belser
Managing Editor Michelle Hope
Art Director & Designer Megan Sinead Bingham
Production Designer Jean Hwang
VP Manufacturing Alix Nicholaeff
Senior Production Manager Joshua Smith
Strategic Production Planner Lina s Palma-Temena

Photographer Stacy Ventura
Food Stylist Victoria Woollard
Food Stylist Assistant Allee Cakmis
Pitmaster Assistant Brian Ventura

Weldon Owen would also like to thank Margaret Parrish and Mary Cassells.

ISBN: 979-8-88674-369-2

Manufactured in China by Insight Editions

10 9 8 7 6 5 4 3 2 1

ROOTS of PEACE REPLANTED PAPER

Insight Editions, in association with Roots of Peace, will plant two trees for each tree used in the manufacturing of this book. Roots of Peace is an internationally renowned humanitarian organization dedicated to eradicating land mines worldwide and converting war-torn lands into productive farms and wildlife habitats. Roots of Peace will plant two million fruit and nut trees in Afghanistan and provide farmers there with the skills and support necessary for sustainable land use.

FLAVOR TRAIN